SECOND EDITION

Workbook

6

Herbert Puchta · Peter Lewis-Jones · Günter Gerngross · Helen Kidd

CAMBRIDGE
UNIVERSITY PRESS

Contents

Back to school

1 Match the words.

1 tennis `c`   a rack
2 basketball [ ]   b pitch
3 school [ ]   c ~~court~~
4 running [ ]   d bin
5 football [ ]   e track
6 bike [ ]   f bell
7 litter [ ]   g hoop

2 Look at the pictures. Write the words.

① _____   ② _____   ③ _____

bike rack   _____   _____

④ _____   ⑤ _____   ⑥ _____

_____   _____   _____

⑦ _____   ⑧ _____   ⑨ _____

_____   _____   _____

3 Complete the dialogue with the words from the box.

ask always strange Science
~~idea~~ day know Tuesday

Patrick So, what lesson have we got now?
Alex I've no (1) ____idea____ .
I don't even (2) _____
what day it is.
Phoebe Neither do I. Look, there's Sam.
Let's (3) _____ her.
Phoebe Hi, Sam.
What (4) _____
is it today?
Sam It's (5) _____ .
Don't you know that?
Alex So, we've got
(6) _____ with
Mr Davis now.
Sam Yes, that's right. We
(7) _____ have
Science on Tuesdays after lunch.
Phoebe Of course.
Sam You guys are (8) _____ !

1 Complete with *yet* or *already*.

Language focus ▶

Hi there, my name's Leo.

Come in and have some fun.

Have you had some food (1) _____?

Are you with someone?

Yes, I know you're Leo.

Because you are my son.

And we have (2) _____ met.

Leo – I'm your mum!

2 Match the sentences from the box with the pictures.

She's already got her new bike.   They've already finished their treehouse.   He hasn't found the answer yet.
~~They haven't finished their treehouse yet.~~   He's already found the answer.   She hasn't got her new bike yet.

They haven't finished their treehouse yet.

_____

_____

_____

_____

_____

3 Make sentences.

1 breakfast / he's / had / already

   He's already had breakfast   .

2 Linda / Brazil / been / yet / to / hasn't

   _____ .

3 haven't / yet / girlfriend / his / I / met

   _____ .

4 we've / seen / that / already / film

   _____ .

4 Write questions.

1 he / phone / Lisa yet?

   Has he phoned Lisa yet? _____

2 you / buy / my present yet?

   _____

3 they / walk / the dog yet?

   _____

4 she / repair / her bike yet?

   _____

1   **001** Do you remember? Read, listen and complete the song with the words from the box.

> walked   fast   past   where   cross   Have
> time   along   talked   lost   ~~been~~   future

They've already (1) ___**been**___ to Pompeii
And seen fights in the old Wild West
And they've been (2) _____ at sea
On board the *Mary Celeste*.

They've already (3) _____ to Elvis
And had some cake in space.
They've (4) _____ in the rainforest –
A really amazing place!

(5) _____ they been to Africa?
Will they go there? Yes or no?
Come (6) _____ and let's find out
The places (7) _____ they'll go.

The Time Travellers –
They're lost in (8) _____.
They'll never come back if they
(9) _____ that line.

The Time Travellers –
Travelling so (10) _____.
The (11) _____ is the present
and the (12) _____ is the past.

2 **002** Listen and say the words.

r**ai**n   d**ay**   c**a**ke

Phonics tip

Look for spelling patterns to help you say words. For example, r**ai**n, d**ay** and c**a**ke all have the same long vowel sound.

3 Say the words from the box and write them in the correct sound column.

> ~~rain~~   ~~team~~   boat   new   table   learn
> right   use   time   person   place   piece
> key   flies   hole   gold   blue   surf

s**ay**	s**ee**	m**y**
rain	team	

kn**ow**	t**oo**	b**ir**d

4 **003** Listen, check and say the words.

 6   Song practice; phonics focus: spelling patterns

1 Complete with *which, who* or *where*.

My name's Leo and I'm a leopard.

I'm the leopard (1) ___who___ likes to rap.

These are the words (2) _____ I rap.

I'll keep rapping while you clap.

This is the jungle (3) _____ I rule.

This is the jungle (4) _____ I'm king.

King of the jungle, king of cool.

You keep clapping while I sing.

2 Look at the pictures. Write the words to complete the sentences.

1 A cook is an example of someone who wears an ___apron___ for work.

2 A _____ _____ is a container where you mix things in a laboratory.

3 My coat pocket is the place where I keep my _____.

4 My model planes are the things which I keep on my bedroom _____.

5 _____ are the things which you wear to protect your eyes.

6 The headteacher is the person who rings the school _____.

3 Complete the sentences with *which, who* or *where*.

1 The running track is the place ___where___ we have our school sports day.

2 The Year 10 boys are the ones _____ spend all lunchtime on the football pitch.

3 The bike rack is the place _____ we leave our bikes.

4 The basketball hoop is the thing _____ we try to jump up and touch.

5 Mrs Henderson is the lunchtime assistant _____ walks around the playground.

6 The school bell at the end of break is the thing _____ I hate most.

4 Complete the sentences so that they are true for you.

1 ___Football___ is something ___which___ I enjoy.

2 _____ is the person _____ I spend most time with.

3 _____ is the place _____ I'd like to be now.

4 _____ is the thing _____ I play with most.

1 🛡️ **Remember the story. Choose five adjectives from the box to complete the summary.**

careful   ill   sorry   worried
excited   ~~happy~~   bored   hungry

The children go into the Science lab. Patrick isn't
(1) ___happy___ because he doesn't like Science. Alex and
Phoebe think that something strange is happening. Then
they see the date and it's the same date as when they
started their adventures. Alex is (2) _____ that it is
all going to happen again. Phoebe says that if they are
(3) _____, they won't have an accident. They decide
that Patrick can't help this time. Alex and Phoebe do all
the same experiments again, while Patrick just watches.
He is (4) _____ and he's fiddling with his goggles.
Mr Davis, the teacher, comes to talk to the children and he
tells Patrick to put his goggles on. The goggles fly out of
Patrick's hand and knock over a jar of powder on the shelf
above the desk. The powder starts falling into the mixture
below. There is a big explosion and Patrick is
(5) _____, but then the yellow light appears.
The children know what they have to do and they walk
through the gate.

2 **Complete the sentences with *which*, *who* or *where*.**

1 The blue powder is the thing ___which___
   causes the explosion.

2 Mr Davis is the man _____ teaches
   them Science.

3 Phoebe and Alex read the instructions
   _____ Mr Davis gave them.

4 The shelf is the place _____ the
   goggles hit the jar.

5 Patrick is the boy _____ causes
   the accident.

6 The Science lab is the room _____
   the accident happens.

3 🛡️ **Choose the best answer for each question.**

1 Why does Alex say, 'This is strange'?
   a Because of the date. ☐
   b Because the Science lesson
     seems the same. ☑️

2 Why does Phoebe say, 'You're not going
   to do any of the experiments!' to Patrick?
   a Because she doesn't want the
     accident to happen again. ☐
   b Because he's not very good
     at Science. ☐

3 Why does Patrick say, 'That's not fair'?
   a Because he really wants to do
     some experiments. ☐
   b Because he thinks the other two
     are being unkind to him. ☐

4 Why does Phoebe say, 'Sit there'
   to Patrick?
   a Because she wants him far away
     from the experiment. ☐
   b Because she needs him to help her. ☐

5 Why does Mr Davis say, 'Excellent' to
   the children?
   a Because they have done some
     really good work. ☐
   b Because Patrick is fiddling with
     his goggles. ☐

6 Why does Phoebe shout, 'What have
   you done?'?
   a Because she doesn't know what
     Patrick has done. ☐
   b Because she is angry with Patrick. ☐

4 What message can we learn from the story? <u>Underline</u> the best value statement.

a Don't put things on high shelves because they can cause accidents.

b Don't fiddle with things because you can cause accidents.

c Don't work with your friends because you'll have an accident.

5 Write a true sentence for each picture from the story with the words from the box.

> children / not / walk / into the light yet ~~lesson / already / start~~
> Patrick / not / knock / the powder over yet   blue powder / already / start / to fall

1 The lesson has already started.

2 _____

3 _____

4 _____

6 Read and think about the situations. What do you think will happen? Complete the chart with two ideas about each situation.

1 Patrick pretends to be ill. He goes to see the school nurse.

2 Patrick doesn't fiddle with his goggles.

3 Patrick sits on a chair and doesn't move for the whole lesson.

4 Mr Davis puts Alex in a different group.

Your ideas	What happens?
1A The nurse gives him some medicine and sends him back to the classroom.	
2A	… so the explosion still happens.
3A	
4A	
1B The nurse sends him home.	
2B	… so the explosion doesn't happen.
3B	
4B	

1 Look at the pictures. Complete the words.

①

t r e a s u r e
c h e s t

②

e _ _ _ _ – p _ _ _ _ c h

③

b _ _ _ o c _ _ _ _ rs

④

p _ _ m t _ _ _ _

⑤

h _ m _ _ c k

⑥

h _ _ e

⑦

c _ _ _ n _

⑧

h _ _ k

⑨

k _ _

⑩

s _ _ d _

2 Do the crossword.

Across
5 ~~There are gold coins in this.~~
7 It's in the ground.
9 You can climb this.
10 A pirate sometimes has this instead of a hand.
11 You dig holes with this.

Down
1 You can see things that are far away with these.
2 These are made of metal. They're money.
3 This is a piece of rock.
4 You can rest or sleep in this.
6 You can open doors (and treasure chests!) with this.
8 You wear this over one eye.

3 Complete the sentences with the words from the box and the past tense of the verbs in brackets.

coin   eye-patch   hammock
~~hole~~   spade   treasure chest

1 Dad _____dug_____ (dig) a big _____hole_____ in the garden.
2 My uncle _____ (wear) an _____ after his accident.
3 I _____ (pass) Mum the _____ and she planted the tree.
4 The pirates _____ (bury) the _____ in the soft sand.
5 I _____ (find) a very old _____ in my money box!
6 We _____ (put) up a _____ between two trees.

1 Read and complete with *for* or *since*.

Language focus

1 I've had these lovely spots _____ I was a cub.

2 I've had my big, long tail _____ eleven years.

2 Complete the chart with the phrases from the box.

> ~~eleven o'clock~~   five years   April   Wednesday   three hours   2015
> the fourteenth century   ten minutes   last week   eight months   yesterday
> an hour   a long time   three weeks   twenty seconds   my birthday

for		since	
_____	_____	eleven o'clock	_____
_____	_____	_____	_____
_____	_____	_____	_____
_____	_____	_____	_____

3 Complete the sentences with *for* or *since*.

1 I've had my bike _____ for _____ six months.

2 I haven't had an email from Zoe _____ Christmas.

3 She hasn't visited her grandparents _____ two weeks.

4 He has known his friend Jack _____ the summer holidays.

5 We haven't eaten anything _____ early this morning.

6 I've known my friend Oliver _____ three years.

4 Write five sentences that are true for you. Use the verbs from the box.

> play   have   live   be interested in   know

I've played the guitar for three years. _____

_____

_____

_____

_____

1 🛡 **Remember the song. Complete the verbs and match.**

1 I've k <u>n</u> <u>o</u> <u>w</u> <u>n</u>　　[e]　　a for gold and silver for years.

2 I've w ___ ___ ___ ___　　[　]　　b a lot of treasure.

3 I've l ___ ___ ___ ___　　[　]　　c to say, 'We're pirates!' in three languages.

4 I've r ___ ___ ___ ___　　[　]　　d lots of ships.

5 I've l ___ ___ ___ ___ ___　　[　]　　e ~~my parrot since she was an egg.~~

6 I've f ___ ___ ___ ___　　[　]　　f around for years on a wooden leg.

2 **Correct the sentences.**

1 The pirate's parrot is called Bonny.　　<u>The pirate's parrot is called Polly.</u>

2 The pirates are in the Arctic.　　_____

3 The pirate speaks German, French and Portuguese.　　_____

4 He's looked for horses and cows.　　_____

5 He's found a lot of treasure on mountains.　　_____

3 🎧 004 **Listen and say the words.**

mi<u>x</u>ture　trea<u>s</u>ure

Phonics tip

Listen to these words. Can you hear the different sounds at the end of mix<u>ture</u> and trea<u>sure</u>?

4 **Complete the sentences with the words from the box. Match them with pictures a–f.**

> future　~~mixture~~　picture　treasure　adventure　measure

1 Put the cake ___<u>mixture</u>___ in the pan. Then put it in the oven.　[d]

2 Do you think cars will be able to fly in the _____?　[　]

3 The pirate's _____ chest is full of gold coins.　[　]

4 Let's take a _____ of the parrots.　[　]

5 The three friends are travelling on an _____ through time.　[　]

6 Use your ruler to _____ the square carefully.　[　]

5 🎧 005 **Listen, check and say the sentences.**

Song practice; phonics focus: -sure and -ture

1 Complete the present perfect questions.

Language focus

How long (1) _____ (have) them?

Since I was thirteen.

How long (2) _____ (be) here?

For eleven weeks.

2 Look at the photos. Write questions and answers.

ten o'clock   six months   two weeks   2010

1 How long / Holly / be / in the park?

   How long has Holly been in the park?   She's been in the park since ten o'clock.

2 How long / the Westalls / have / their dog?

   _____   _____

3 How long / Charlie / have / his phone?

   _____   _____

4 How long / the Andersons / live / in this house?

   _____   _____

3 Read the poem. Then write your own.

How long have you had your old blue bike?

   For five years, for five years.

How long have you had your old red ball?

   Since I was seven, since I was seven.

How long have you had your old green cap?

   Since I was six, since I was six.

OK, fine. Let's go into town.

You need new stuff. Let's go and buy it now.

_____
_____
_____
_____
_____

OK, fine. Let's go into town.

You need new stuff. Let's go and buy it now.

1 Remember the story. Number these objects in the order they appear in the story.

a ☐ b ☐ c [1] d ☐ e ☐ f ☐

2 Read the summary. Find five more mistakes.

Through their binoculars, the children watch the pirates sail away. They also see another ship with green sails and a black flag. When they look to the south, they see a bigger island with a town on it. Then they go to dig up the treasure. After three hours, they find the chest which is full of gold coins. While they are deciding what to do with the treasure, they see some people with children arriving. They bring coconuts and talk to the people, who explain that the pirates have stolen their gold.

The children show them the treasure and give it back to them. They tell the people to go to the town on the other island. The people then leave.

Later, at night, five pirates and their prisoner arrive. They are looking for the treasure, but they only find a big hole. Patrick sneezes and the pirates find the children. The pirates want to know where the chest has gone and they threaten to throw the children into the sea. Then the light appears in the hole, so the children jump in and escape.

a ship with red sails
_____   _____
_____   _____
_____   _____

3 Match the questions with the answers.

1 Why did the children run to see the people in the boat? [e]
2 Why did the children hide from the people shouting? ☐
3 Where was the ship with the black flag going to? ☐
4 Where was the island with the town on it? ☐
5 When did the children drink some coconut milk? ☐
6 When did Phoebe and Patrick start arguing? ☐
7 What did the children give the people? ☐
8 What did the children give the pirates? ☐

a The north.
b Before they dug the hole.
c The treasure chest.
d Nothing!
e ~~Because they weren't pirates.~~
f The south.
g After they dug the hole.
h Because they were pirates.

4 Write the events from the story in the correct order to show the times when they happened.

> The children go to sleep.   The pirates finish and leave the island.
> The children welcome the families to the island.   The children find the treasure.
> The children jump into the hole.   The children start digging for the treasure.
> The children hear shouting.   The children watch the pirates burying the treasure.
> The children say goodbye to the families.   ~~The children arrive on the island.~~

8.45 a.m.	The children arrive on the island.
9 a.m.	
10 a.m.	
11 a.m.	
1 p.m.	
1.30 p.m.	
3.30 p.m.	
8 p.m.	
midnight	
12.15 a.m.	

5 Read and complete the time phrases. Use the information from Activity 4.

1 It's 9.45 a.m. The pirates have been at the hole …
for __45 minutes__
since __9 a.m.__ .

2 It's 11.25 a.m. The children haven't seen the pirates …
for _____
since _____ .

3 It's 1.15 p.m. The children have had the treasure …
for _____
since _____ .

4 It's 3.05 p.m. They have been with the families …
for _____
since _____ .

5 It's 7.45 p.m. They have been on the island …
for _____
since _____ .

6 It's 11.55 p.m. The children have been asleep …
for _____
since _____ .

6 Imagine the families don't come to the island. What should the children do with the treasure? Write b (best), o (OK) and w (worst) next to the three ideas. Think of two more good ideas.

1 Leave it on the island. ☐   2 Keep it and spend it on toys, sweets and games. ☐   3 Give it to the local hospital. ☐

_____

_____

1 Read the article in the Student's Book again. Complete the questions.

1 ___What___ is the sword made of?

2 _____ found it?

3 _____ did she think it was at first?

4 _____ is the sword so special?

5 _____ are they going to put the sword?

6 _____ did Saga move to Sweden?

2 Match the questions from Activity 1 with the answers.

a ☐ It's very old – maybe 1,500 years old.

b ☐ An 8-year-old girl who was throwing stones across a lake.

c ☐ A year ago.

d ☐1☐ It's made of metal, wood and leather.

e ☐ A stick.

f ☐ In the museum, for everyone to see.

3 Read the dialogue and choose the best answer. Write letters A–H. There are two extra answers.

Emma What are you doing today?

Nick (1) _D_

Emma Why do you want to go there? It's cold!

Nick (2) ___

Emma Wow! And what did he do with the necklace?

Nick (3) ___

Emma How silly of him!

Nick (4) ___

Emma Really? Right, I've got to go. I'm in a hurry.

Nick (5) ___

Emma To the beach!

Nick (6) ___

A Why? Where are you going?

B I'm going to the park.

C He reported his find to a big museum.

D ~~I'm thinking of going to the beach.~~

E Because our neighbour found an old gold necklace buried in the sand on the beach.

F Right! Let's go together!

G He gave it to his wife for her birthday.

H It wasn't! It was the honest thing to do. They gave him €5,000.

1 Complete the five conversations. Choose A, B or C.

1 Guess what? I found a golden bracelet.

  A I hope so too.   B Really? How exciting!   C I want it too.

2 Can you show me your new bracelet?

  A It's expensive.   B You're welcome.   C Yes, sure.

3 How long have you had the bracelet?

  A It took three months.   B For two weeks.   C Last month.

4 I'm sorry, I can't tell you the price.

  A What a pity!   B I hope so.   C I'll take two.

5 I'm sorry, I don't like your suggestion.

  A OK, let's make it then.   B I didn't like it.   C OK, let's think of a better idea.

2 Write the beginning of an interview between a radio presenter and someone who has found a valuable object. Use your ideas from Student's Book page 17.

_____
_____
_____
_____
_____
_____

3 🎧 006 Listen and write.

Treasures and mysteries

Meetings after school on:	(1) __Thursdays__
Children learn about:	(2) _____
They look at:	special (3) _____
Teacher's friend works at:	the (4) _____
Children may have to wear:	(5) _____
Teacher who leads club:	Miss (6) _____

Think and learn

1 Look and write the labels.

gold ~~gold mine~~ rock silver

a

gold mine

b

_____

c

_____

d

_____

2 Read and tick ☑ the true sentences.

Where in the world can we find gold and silver ?

Gold is found all over the world, but some countries produce more gold than others. For many years, South Africa produced the most gold, but now it's the sixth-largest producer of gold because mining is more difficult. Silver is also found all over the world. Mexico produced the most silver for a long time, but in the last few years, China has opened more silver mines, as well as gold mines. China now produces the most gold in the world and is the second-largest producer of silver. Peru has more silver in the ground than any other country. One day, it could produce more silver than Mexico.

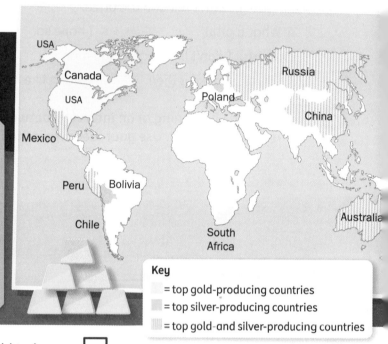

Key
░ = top gold-producing countries
▓ = top silver-producing countries
▥ = top gold-and silver-producing countries

1 South Africa produces the most gold in the world today. ☐

2 China produces more gold and silver now than it used to. ☐

3 Peru produces more silver than Mexico. ☐

4 Mexico produces the most silver in the world today. ☐

3 🛡 Look and complete the chart with the names of the countries from the map in Activity 2.

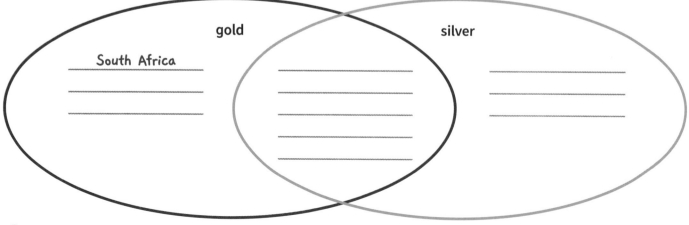

gold

silver

South Africa

4 Look and think. Why are silver and gold used in these objects?

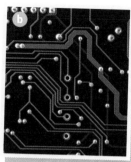

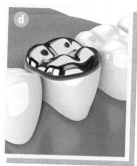

5 Read and complete the sentences. Then match them with the objects from Activity 4.

Silver and gold are precious for many reasons. They don't react with many other things and they are also not affected by water. Gold is not affected by the air, but the surface of silver can sometimes become black. Both gold and silver reflect light, so they look shiny. They are soft metals and easy to make lots of different things with. Gold can be stretched into thin layers or even into wires. It can be melted and mixed with other metals to make it harder. Silver and gold can also carry electricity and heat very well.

electricity   Gold   light   ~~precious~~   soft

1 [c] Gold and silver are ____precious____ metals.

2 [ ] _____ is not affected by water or air.

3 [ ] Gold and silver reflect _____.

4 [ ] Gold and silver are _____ and easy to make things with.

5 [ ] Gold and silver can carry _____ and heat.

6 ⭐ Project What did you find out? Complete the chart.

	gold	silver
What is made from it?		
Where is it found?		
What is it like?		

1 Draw lines and complete the sentences with the words from the box.

since I   long have   seen Sue   in your   ~~for eight~~   mum has

1 We've lived	worked at the	_for eight_ years.
2 I've had	you known	was six.
3 My _____	in London	hospital since 1998.
4 Tom hasn't	my dog _____	Mr Lester?
5 How _____	has Mary lived	six months.
6 How long	_____ for	_____ street?

2 Find the words and use them to complete the sentences.

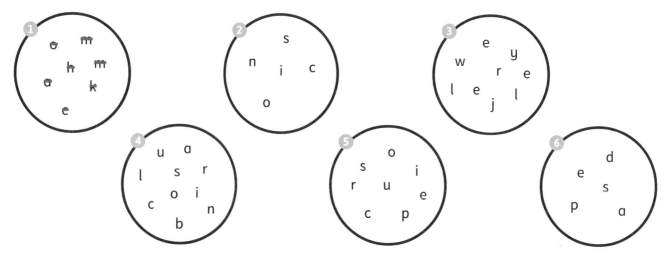

1 My dad loves to relax in his _____ hammock _____ in the garden on a sunny afternoon.
2 Do you have any _____? I need some to buy coffee from the machine.
3 My favourite piece of _____ is this necklace.
4 If you look through the _____, you can read what it says on that plane.
5 Gold and silver are known as _____ metals.
6 If you want to dig a really deep hole, you'll need a bigger _____.

3 Complete the sentences with your own ideas.

1 I've known _____.
2 _____ for a year.
3 How long have _____?
4 How long has _____?

What do I know?

1 Read and tick ✓. Then write examples.

1 I can use the present perfect with *for* and *since*. ☐

I have _____ for _____.

_____ has _____ since _____.

2 I can write questions with *How long have you …* ? ☐

_____

3 I can write the names of five things that pirates use. ☐

_____ _____ _____

_____ _____

2 🛡 Write sentences to answer the Big Question. **BIG QUESTION** What kinds of treasure are there?

_____
_____
_____
_____

My story

3 Look at the pictures and write a story about a boy called Luke.

Luke was very excited ..._____
_____
_____
_____
_____
_____
_____
_____
_____
_____
_____
_____

1 Find eight more transport gadgets. Draw lines to the correct pictures. There is one extra picture.

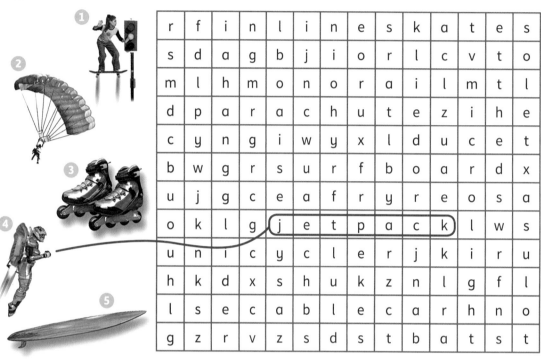

r	f	i	n	l	i	n	e	s	k	a	t	e	s
s	d	a	g	b	j	i	o	r	l	c	v	t	o
m	l	h	m	o	n	o	r	a	i	l	m	t	l
d	p	a	r	a	c	h	u	t	e	z	i	h	e
c	y	n	g	i	w	y	x	l	d	u	c	e	t
b	w	g	r	s	u	r	f	b	o	a	r	d	x
u	j	g	c	e	a	f	r	y	r	e	o	s	a
o	k	l	g	j	e	t	p	a	c	k	l	w	s
u	n	i	c	y	c	l	e	r	j	k	i	r	u
h	k	d	x	s	h	u	k	z	n	l	g	f	l
l	s	e	c	a	b	l	e	c	a	r	h	n	o
g	z	r	v	z	s	d	s	t	b	a	t	s	t

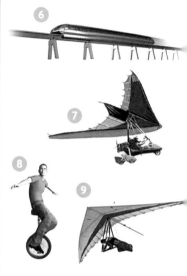

2 Complete the chart with words from Activity 1.

Transport gadgets	for one person in the air	floating skateboard
	for one person on the ground or water	
	for more than one person	

3 Complete the sentences with words from the box.

> monorail   solar panels   surfboard   ~~unicycle~~
> parachute   Wind turbines   cable car

1 My uncle works in a circus. He rides a ____unicycle____ and juggles balls.

2 He jumped from the plane and opened his _____.

3 Take the _____ direct from the airport. It's the quickest way into the city.

4 You can get to the top of the mountain in three hours, or in ten minutes by _____.

5 The shark took a big bite out of his _____.

6 _____ and _____ are gadgets that make energy.

1 Put the words in the correct order.

Language focus

1 a / You / here / car / don't / get / round / to / need / about / drive / to

_____.

2 catch / to / need / to / You / round / bus / don't / about / here/ a / get

_____.

2 Complete the sentences with *need to* or *don't need to*.

1 We leave at six. You ____need to____ be at school at ten to six.

2 You _____ call Lucy. I've already called her.

3 You _____ bring any snacks with you. We'll have lunch at a restaurant.

4 You're cold, aren't you? You _____ wear a thicker jumper.

5 You _____ do the washing up. We've got a dishwasher.

6 I feel sick. I _____ go to the bathroom.

7 The fridge is empty. We _____ do some shopping.

8 You _____ help your brother. He can't do his homework and I don't speak German.

3 Look at the advert. What do you need to bring?

FOR THE GREATEST ADVENTURE,
JOIN OUR 2-DAY CAVE TRIP!

BRING:

For the cave trip, you _____
_____
_____
_____
_____
_____
_____
_____
_____

4 Write a sentence for each picture.

1 You don't need to put up the tent. I'll do it for you.

2 _____

3 _____

4 _____

1 Complete the dialogue with words from the box.

> need   to   Cool   silly   don't   present   ~~riding~~   Really

Charlie   Wow, Holly – what are you (1) _____riding_____ ?

Holly   It's my new unicycle. It was a (2) _____ for my birthday.

Charlie   (3) _____ ?

Holly   Yes. I've wanted one for ages.

Charlie   (4) _____ ! Do you (5) _____ to wear a helmet with it?

Holly   I don't think so. I (6) _____ ride it on the road.

Charlie   I know, but if you fall, you could hurt your head.

Holly   But I look (7) _____ in a helmet.

Charlie   You don't look silly. You need (8) _____ be safe!

2 (🎧 007) Listen and say the words.

televi*sion*   sta*tion*   profe*ssion*

Phonics tip

The *-ion* syllable isn't stressed, so it has a short vowel sound. Most words ending in *-sion* have the same sound as in televi*sion*. Most words ending in *-tion* or *-ssion* have the *sh* sound.

3 Complete the sentences with words from the box.

> instructions   ~~station~~   explosion   emission
> television   pollution   revision   invitation

Word watch

ques*tion* is pronounced with a *ch* sound

1 I went to the _____station_____ to catch the nine o'clock train.

2 Cars in the future will be _____ -free.

3 Jack watched _____ after he finished his homework.

4 If you want to use that machine, please read the _____ carefully.

5 I need to do some _____ before the Science exam next week.

6 Julie gave me an _____ to her birthday party on Saturday.

7 If you mix those powders together, you'll cause an _____ .

8 There's a lot of _____ in big cities.

4 (🎧 008) Listen, check and say the sentences.

1 **Read and match.**

Language focus

1 There will be a lot of noise   as quickly as they can.

2 There won't be any trees left   have got a plan.

3 I won't let that happen. I   when the diggers come.

4 They'll have to run away   after the workers go.

2 **Make sentences about what *will* or *won't* happen in the future.**

1 will / trees / cities / be / in / there / lots / of / our There will be lots of trees in our cities.

2 there / any / cars / won't / be / drivers / with _____.

3 cities / most / have / will / monorails _____.

4 won't / car / be / any / accidents / there _____.

5 people / in / eat / fast- / restaurants / will / pills / food _____.

6 will / people / more / have / play / time / to _____.

3 **What will the world be like in 2050? Look at the pictures and write sentences.**

1 There will be cities on the moon _____.

2 There won't be _____.

3 Children _____.

4 Students _____.

5 Children _____.

6 Cars _____.

1 Remember the story. Put the sentences in order.

☐ Patrick's parachute opens.

☐ Phoebe and Alex shout instructions to Patrick.

☐ Phoebe and Alex fly around the mountain.

☐ They fly over the park and towards the sea.

☐ The man congratulates Patrick on good flying.

1 Phoebe and Alex read the instructions carefully.

☐ Phoebe starts to get worried about Patrick.

☐ They see Patrick falling through the sky.

2 Complete the chart.

Who?	How do they feel?	When?
(1) Phoebe and Alex	(2) nervous	they read the instructions
(3) _____	excited	(4) _____
(5) _____	(6) _____	she can't see Patrick anywhere
(7) _____	scared	(8) _____

3 Complete the jet pack instructions with the correct colours from the story.

Congratulations on buying the

Flyme X2000!

Before you take to the skies, please take the time to read and remember:

To take off, press the (1) _____yellow_____ button.

To go higher, press the (2) _____ button.

To go faster, press the (3) _____ button.

To go down, press the (4) _____ button.

To open the parachute, press the

(5) _____ and the (6) _____

buttons together.

Fly safely and enjoy yourself!

4   **What message can we learn from the story in the Student's Book? <u>Underline</u> the best value statement.**

a If you think you know how to use something, you don't need to read the instructions.

b You should always read the instructions before you use something new.

c Some people don't need to read the instructions before they use something new.

5 **Look at the photos. Complete the sentences.**

~~traffic~~ go surfing teacher ~~cross the road~~ instructor lifeguard

use a parachute do her homework

1 They need to <u>look and listen carefully to the traffic before they cross the road</u>.

2 She needs to _____.

3 He needs to _____.

4 They need to _____.

6 **Write about two more situations where you need to listen carefully.**

You need to listen carefully to the rules when you play a game.

_____

_____

7 **Complete the sentences so that they are true for you.**

1 I need to listen carefully when _____ because _____.

2 I didn't listen carefully when _____ , so _____.

1  **Listen to five short conversations. Tick ☑ the right answer. There is one example.**

1   Where did Brenda's family go on holiday last year?

a Spain	b Turkey	c Italy
	 ☑	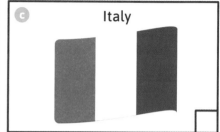

2   How many postcards did the man buy?

a	b	c

3   What time does Sue's piano lesson start?

a	b	c

4   How far is Jane's nearest train station?

a	b	c

5   What will the weather be like?

a	b	c
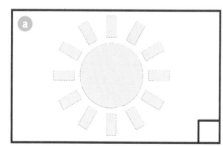		

1 Read the sentences. Complete the information on the leaflet.

a You need to be 17 to hire the most expensive thing.

b Floating skateboards cost €5 an hour.

c Inline skates are €7 cheaper than surfboards.

d You can hire floating skateboards and surfboards at the same age.

e If you are nine, you can hire inline skates. If you are eight, you can't hire anything.

f You need to be 13 to hire the things that cost €15 an hour.

g Unicycles are three times more expensive than inline skates.

h Microlights cost €15 more than inline skates.

i A nine-year-old needs to be two years older to hire floating skateboards.

j Surfboards cost €12 an hour.

FOR HIRE

- Microlights: € (1) _____ an hour (minimum age (2) _____)
- Floating skateboards: € (3) ___5___ an hour (minimum age (4) _____)
- Unicycles: € (5) _____ an hour (minimum age (6) _____)
- Inline skates: € (7) _____ an hour (minimum age (8) _____)
- Surfboards: € (9) _____ an hour (minimum age (10) _____)

2 Read and complete with a word from the box. There are four extra words.

sea   carried   boat   jet   minutes   ~~cross~~   earlier   land   journey   last

In August 2019, a French inventor became the first person to (1) ____cross____ the English Channel on a 'flyboard' or 'hoverboard' – a board powered by a (2) _____ pack. Franky Zapata crossed the Channel on a board he made himself. It took him just 20 (3) _____ to travel from Sangatte, in northern France, to Dover, in England. The board had five turbines and was powered by fuel in the inventor's backpack. He (4) _____ enough fuel for 10 minutes, so halfway through the (5) _____, he needed to land on a boat to pick up more fuel for the second half. The first time Franky tried to cross the Channel, two weeks (6) _____, he fell into the sea!

1 Look and write.   solar panels   solar-powered plane   ~~wind turbines~~   battery   biofuel

a wind turbines   b _____   c _____   d _____   e _____

2 Match the definitions with the words from Activity 1.

1 [d] Many electronic games and toys need these to work.

2 [ ] This is made from natural materials from trees and crops.

3 [ ] One of these has flown around the world.

4 [ ] These collect energy from the sun.

5 [ ] These make electricity from a natural source. They can be on land or in the sea.

3 Read and write *true* or *false*.

RENEWABLE ENERGY

PAST, PRESENT AND FUTURE

We are using more renewable energy now than ever before, but it isn't a new idea.

Windmills were made in Iran over 2,000 years ago and the Romans used warm air from the earth, called geothermal energy, under their floors to heat their homes.

Today, in the UK, almost one third of the electricity used comes from renewable sources. Solar power can be used even when the sun isn't shining because it can be stored in salt and then used at night.

In 2016, the whole country of Portugal used only renewable energy for 107 hours in a row – amazing!

Scientists think it's possible that solar power will be the world's main source of power by 2050. They also say it's possible that Europe and North Africa will be able to use 100% renewable energy by then.

1 Renewable energy was used for the first time in the 20th century.   _____false_____

2 Solar power, wind and biofuel are the only forms of renewable energy.   _____

3 Around 30% of the UK's electricity comes from renewable energy.   _____

4 You can use energy from solar power in the day and at night.   _____

5 In 2050, Europe and North Africa might use only renewable energy.   _____

4   Read about two more types of renewable energy. Match the advantages and disadvantages (1–6) to each one.

Energy from the
EARTH & WATER

The Earth's natural heat and the power of water are two more types of renewable energy. As well as being renewable, they are both very clean sources of energy, and they can be found in many different parts of the world. In fact, 100% of Iceland's energy comes from the Earth and from water.

These are not new ideas: people have used the Earth's natural heat since Roman times. The Ancient Greeks used the power of water to move water wheels in mills that made flour. Nowadays, water is stored in large man-made lakes, called dams, and the energy from the moving water is changed into electricity.

1 Can cause problems for fish in the environment.
2 Can be used to make people's homes warm.
3 Can provide a place for people to swim and go on boats.
4 Doesn't depend on the weather.
5 Can help to control floods.
6 Can cause earthquakes.

Energy from the Earth   **Energy from water**

 ☐   ☐

☐   ☐

 ☐   1

5   Look, read and complete the information.

ARE YOU READY FOR A
WIND-POWERED CAR?

Is it a bike? Is it a car? It's a ventomobile!

It uses a wind turbine for power.

It doesn't go fast, but it only uses energy from the wind.

Will this be the future of car travel?

The (1) __ventomobile__ was invented in 2008 by a group of university students.

It had three (2) _____ and it looked more like a

(3) _____ than a car.

Its power comes from a two-metre (4) _____ on top.

It was probably the first car to use only the power of the (5) _____.

1 Correct the sentences by writing the missing words from the box in the right place.

don't   won't   to   ~~will~~   need   use

1 There be too many cars in the world soon.
   There will be too many cars in the world soon   .

2 You to take a passport to travel to another country.
   _____ .

3 Don't worry, the exam be difficult.
   _____ .

4 Everyone will solar panels for energy one day.
   _____ .

5 You need to say sorry. It wasn't your fault.
   _____ .

6 I want a new computer. I need talk to Dad.
   _____ .

2 Join the parts to make words and use them to complete the sentences.

bat   in   mono   para   ~~surf~~   tur

bines   ~~board~~   chute   line   rail   tery

1 You must be good at swimming if you want to take a _____*surfboard*_____ into the sea.
2 Wind _____ can be around 100 metres tall.
3 When are they going to build a _____ in our city?
4 Patrick pressed the two buttons and opened his _____ .
5 I love my electric bike. When I'm tired, I use the _____ !
6 I had some _____ skates for my birthday.

3 Complete the sentences with your own ideas.

1 There will _____ .
2 I won't _____ .
3 It's cold outside. You need _____ .
4 You don't _____ . I've already done it.

1 **Read and tick ☑. Then write examples.**

What do I know?

1 I can use *need to* and *don't need to* correctly. ☐

_____

_____

2 I can use *will* and *won't* correctly. ☐

_____

_____

3 I can write the names of five transport gadgets. ☐

_____ _____ _____

_____ _____

2 🛡 **Write sentences to answer the Big Question.** **BIG QUESTION** How will people travel in the future?

_____

_____

_____

_____

3 🛡 **Write about school life in 2100.**

My school

Think about: what the lessons will be like.

what the teacher will be like.

what you will still need to do.

what you won't need to do any more.

_____

_____

_____

_____

_____

_____

_____

_____

3 Ancient Egypt

1 Complete the words and match them with the pictures.

1 r _o_ c k   [i]

2 t __ m b   [ ]

3 c h __ r __ __ t   [ ]

4 p h __ r __ __ h   [ ]

5 h __ __ __ r __ g l y p h __ c s   [ ]

6 p y r __ m __ d   [ ]

7 m __ m m y   [ ]

8 S p h __ n x   [ ]

9 s l __ v __ s   [ ]

2 Find four words in Activity 1 to match the definitions.

1 This is a large building in Ancient Egypt.   <u>   pyramid   </u>

2 This is the place where a pharaoh's dead body is buried.   <u>   </u>

3 This is a body covered in bandages. You also see this on scary films.   <u>   </u>

4 This is a kind of writing used by the Ancient Egyptians.   <u>   </u>

3 Complete the dialogue with the words from the box.

> blocks   Sphinx   Pharaoh   step   rock   king   ~~Egypt~~   slaves   chariot

Alex   Look! We're in (1) _____ Egypt _____!

Patrick   The pyramids … and the (2) _____!

Phoebe   I can't believe it! I've always wanted to see the pyramids.

Alex   Who's that man riding on the (3) _____?

Phoebe   He's the (4) _____. He's a kind of (5) _____.

Alex   And look at all those (6) _____! That looks like very hard work.

Patrick   Yes. I hope they don't find us. I don't want to be pulling giant (7) _____

of (8) _____. Come on, let's sit over there on the (9) _____.

1 **Read and complete.**   weren't built   ~~was … built~~   was put in   was built

1 Who _____was_____ this den _____built_____ by? It isn't very strong.

2 The walls _____ so well. The windows are all wrong.

3 The door _____ upside down. The roof is not so strong.

4 This den _____ by monkeys. It won't be here for long.

2 **Complete the dialogue with the past passive of the verbs in brackets.**

Tourist   These igloos are fantastic. How were they made?

Guide   Well, the first thing was to find some hard snow.
Blocks of hard snow (1) ____were cut____ (cut) and
the blocks (2) _____ (put) on sledges.

Tourist   And how did the sledges get here?

Guide   The sledges with the blocks of hard snow (3) _____ (pull) here by dogs.

Tourist   I see. And then?

Guide   The blocks of snow (4) _____ (make) into a spiral shape and the spiral
(5) _____ (build) higher and higher. The men made that little tunnel as an entrance
and then the last few blocks (6) _____ (move) into the igloo through the entrance
and they (7) _____ (lift) up to form the roof. Finally, the spaces between the blocks
(8) _____ (fill) with snow.

3 **Why wasn't Mum happy when she arrived home? Look at the photos and write sentences with the past passive of the verbs from the box.**

sweep   ~~feed~~   tidy   wash

1 The dog wasn't fed.

2 _____

3 _____

4 _____

1 🔄 🎧 010 **Remember the song. Put the sentences in order.**

☐ The boy and the girl closed the lid of the tomb.

☐ They met a pharaoh and talked to him.

☐ The boy and the girl ran out of the shop.

☐ 1 A boy and a girl went to a shop in old Cairo.

☐ The mummy got into the ancient tomb.

☐ They found an old mummy in the shop.

☐ The boy and the girl ran to a pyramid.

☐ When the mummy came to life, they were scared.

☐ They hid in a dark place behind an ancient tomb.

☐ The mummy entered the pyramid.

2 **Imagine and write what happened half an hour later.**

Half an hour later, the mummy ...

_____

3 🎧 011 **Listen and say the words.**

deci_d_ed   pain_t_ed   jumped   arrived

Phonics tip

The -ed ending sounds like a *t* or a *d*. We only say *id* if the last sound before the -ed is a *t* or a *d*.

Just landed

4 **Change the verbs in the box to the past simple. Say them and write them in the correct sound column.**

| ~~cook~~   ~~wait~~   ~~carry~~   agree   need   try |
| finish   shout   stop   land   miss   follow |
| decide   like   visit   enjoy   fix   prepare |

/t/	/d/	/id/
cooked	carried	waited

Word watch

We write *enjoyed* and *played*, but in words with a consonant before the *y*, we must change the *y* to *i*: *hurry – hurried   try – tried*

5 🎧 012 **Listen, check and say the words.**

1 Read and complete.

few   little   lot   ~~lots~~

> **Language focus**
>
> There were (1)_____**lots**_____ of trees in this jungle a (2)_____ years ago.
>
> But in a (3)_____ time, a (4)_____ of them have gone.
>
> We've got to get together to stop this jungle theft,
>
> Before it's far too late and there's nothing left.

2 Complete the sentences and match them with the pictures.

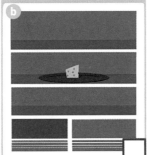

1 There was only __*a little*__ water in the pool.

2 There was _____ cheese in the fridge.

3 There were only _____ people at the concert.

4 There was _____ food in the fridge.

5 There were _____ people at the concert.

3 Look at the pictures and write sentences.

1 There are lots of frogs in the pool.

2 _____.

3 _____.

4 _____.

1 Remember the story. What does Phoebe think about these things?

1 She _____ .

2 _____ .

3 _____ .

2 Read and complete the summary. Copy the missing letters into the spaces below the picture to find out the name of the Pharaoh.

T _ _ _ _ _ _ _ _ _ _ _

The children walk into the pyramid. (1) **T** hey stop to look at some hieroglyphics, but they don't know what they mean. Patrick goes inside first and the other two follow him. It's very dark and after a few (2) min___tes, Phoebe screams when something falls on her head. They look around and see (3) lo___s of scorpions. They (4) st___rt to (5) ru___ down a corridor and they come to a wall. Patrick pushes a button and the floor disappears, so they fall and slide down a long tunnel. They are now in a large, (6) dar___ room. Then Phoebe (7) ___ears something. They all look to where she is pointing and they see a mummy walking towards them. They run towards a light, which is in a (8) sm___ller room, and they block the door with a rock. When they look around, they see that the room is full of beautiful objects. Phoebe realises that it is a (9) to___b and she's happy to stay and look at the treasure, (10) b___t (11) the___ the gate appears.

3 Write *t* (true), *pt* (probably true) or *f* (false).

1 Patrick is the one who wants to go into the pyramid the most. → t

2 Alex isn't scared of bugs like scorpions. → ☐

3 The button makes the floor disappear. → ☐

4 Patrick thinks that it's Alex's fault that they are in the large, dark room. → ☐

5 Phoebe is the first to see the mummy. → ☐

6 Phoebe wants to get out of the room with the treasure. → ☐

4 🛡 This sign in hieroglyphs tells the children how to escape from the tomb. What do you think it says?

a Exit ☐

b Way out ☐

c This way ☐

d Follow me ☐

5 Look at the photos. Complete the holiday advert with the correct form of the words for four of the photos.

FLY TO EGYPT

Let us take you on a magical trip into the past – to a time when
(1) _____pharaohs_____ ruled the land and rode around in golden
(2) _____. Meet the (3) _____, half
woman, half lion. Visit the Egyptian Museum and see the
wonderful treasures that were found in the (4) _____
of kings and queens in the pyramids.

Egypt: Bring your imagination to life!

6 🛡 Choose a country where you or the Time Travellers have been. Write a short advert for it.

Fly to _____!

Let us take you _____.

Meet the _____.

Visit _____

_____.

1 Read the article about Tutankhamun. Choose the best word (A, B or C) for each space. There is one example.

Tutankhamun (1) _____**was**_____ probably born in the Ancient Egyptian capital, called Akhetaten, in the year 1341 BCE. When he was nine years old, he (2) _____ the ruler of Egypt. However, he was only the Pharaoh for a (3) _____ years because he died when he was 18. No-one is sure why he died so young. Some historians think that he was (4) _____ and others think that he died because of an illness. Not very much (5) _____ known about him until 1922, when a famous archaeologist called Howard Carter found his tomb in the Valley of the Kings (6) _____ Egypt. This discovery was very exciting (7) _____ the tomb, which you can see in this photo, was in almost perfect condition. It contained lots of wonderful treasures, including Tutankhamun's beautiful mask. Historians read the hieroglyphs and found out (8) _____ things about this boy pharaoh. These days, you can see many of the treasures on display in the Egyptian Museum in Cairo.

1 A is	(B) was	C were
2 A lived	B became	C got
3 A little	B lot of	C few
4 A murdered	B murder	C murdering
5 A is	B was	C are
6 A in	B on	C up
7 A so	B but	C because
8 A much	B how	C many

2 Read and circle the correct words.

Sign language was invented for people who can't (1) (hear) / see. Deaf people can (2) **hear / communicate** by using sign language. For example, to say *like*, you make a circle with your second finger and your (3) **knee / thumb**. Signing for the deaf on TV (4) **sounds loud / helps people**.

Reading skills; value: respecting differences

1 (013) **Listen to the story from the Student's Book again and complete the sentences.**

1 Rhodopis was a ___servant___ in the old man's house.
2 The other girls felt _____ of Rhodopis.
3 Rhodopis liked to _____ by the river.
4 Rhodopis' shoes were a beautiful _____ colour.
5 A messenger brought news of a _____.
6 A big _____ carried Rhodopis' shoe away.
7 The Pharaoh sat on a _____.
8 Rhodopis became the _____ of Egypt.

2 **Think about the story and complete the chart. You can use the words more than once.**

Rhodopis   birds and a hippo   the bird   everyone   Pharoah

old man   a hippo   one of the girls

Who says …	… these words …	… and who to?
(1) _one of the girls_	'Hurry up, you lazy girl. There's still lots of work to do.'	(2) _Rhodopis_
(3) _____	'I bought these for you.'	(4) _____
(5) _____	'Ha ha! I'm going to the party.'	(6) _____
(7) _____	'Why are they always so mean to me?'	(8) _____
(9) _____	'Careful! You've made my shoes wet.'	(10) _____
(11) _____	'Hey! Where are you going? That's my shoe!'	(12) _____
(13) _____	'I have to find who this shoe belongs to.'	(14) _____
(15) _____	'Will you marry me?'	(16) _____

3 **Read and answer the questions.**

Do you know another story about a girl who is like Rhodopis?
What's the girl's name in your language? Why is she like Rhodopis?

_____
_____
_____
_____

1 Look and write.

> sculpture   papyrus   ~~ceramic pot~~   bright colours   pale colours

ceramic pot

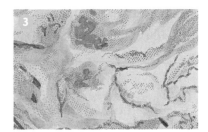

2 What can you remember about Ancient Egyptian art? Read and write *Artists*, *Pharoahs* or *Sculptures*.

1 _____Sculptures_____ were often painted in bright colours.

2 _____ always looked taller than other people in paintings.

3 _____ used a special liquid from trees to keep colours bright.

4 _____ often showed important people sitting down.

5 _____ were always painted in blue and gold.

6 _____ made ceramic pots in lots of different colours.

3 Read and complete the sentences.

> colours   expensive   pale   ~~cats~~   Papyrus   crowns

1 There are lots of sculptures of _____cats_____ in Ancient Egyptian art.

2 Pharaohs often wore _____.

3 _____ was made from the stems of water plants.

4 Egyptian artists painted with six different _____.

5 Blue and gold paints were _____.

6 Hot sun could make bright colours _____.

4 🛡 **What do you think the pictures tell us about life in Ancient Egypt? Look and tick ✓.**

☐ Everyone wore white clothes.

☐ There were doctors in Ancient Egypt.

☐ People ate a lot of rice.

☐ Important people wore white clothes.

☐ Men and women had the same jobs.

☐ People made and ate bread.

5 **Read and check. Were your ideas in Activity 4 right? Match the pictures.**

Ancient Egyptian life and art

We already know that cats were important to the Ancient Egyptians, but what else can we learn about their daily life from their art?

[c] Men and women had different jobs. Men usually worked outside, while women worked indoors at home. In paintings, women often have paler skin than men, to show this difference.

☐ Although most people wore very plain, simple clothes, Egyptian art often shows kings and queens wearing long, bright white clothes. This shows how important they were.

☐ Bread was one of the most important foods in Ancient Egypt, and everyone ate a lot of it. They also ate lots of vegetables and fish. Many sculptures and paintings show people making bread.

☐ In Ancient Egypt, doctors were thought to be the best in the whole world. There are paintings on papyrus of doctors treating patients.

6 ⭐ Project **Look, think and write. What do the colours of the crowns mean?**

① clean and strong ② angry and clean ③ happy and _____ ④ _____ and _____ ⑤ _____ and _____

1 Make three sentences with the phrases in the diamond.
Use three different phrases in each sentence.

1 We were _____
   _____ .

2 _____
   _____ .

3 _____
   _____ .

Diamond phrases:
at the party
on the mountains
lots of people
We were (crossed out)
There were
a dog
There was
a little snow
chased by

2 Find the words and use them to complete the sentences.

1 The sign says to be careful of _____rocks_____ falling from the mountain.

2 _____ were the rulers of Ancient Egypt.

3 There were some beautiful _____ pots in the museum.

4 My older brother wants me to tidy our room, but he made the mess and I'm not his _____!

5 The rich people in Ancient Egypt travelled in _____ .

6 _____ was an early type of paper.

Circles:
1 k o c e r s
2 r a h P o a h s
3 c i r m a c e e
4 l e v a s
5 c i h a t s o r
6 s P u y a r p

3 Complete the sentences with your own ideas.

1 _____ were eaten _____ .

2 _____ by the teacher.

3 I've got lots _____ .

4 There were _____ at _____ .

My Super Mind 3

What do I know?

1 Read and tick ☑. Then write examples.

1 I can use the past passive. ☐

_____

2 I can use *a lot of / lots of / a few / a little*. ☐

_____

_____

_____

3 I can write the names of five things from Ancient Egypt. ☐

_____ _____ _____

_____ _____

2 🛡 Write sentences to answer the Big Question.

BIG QUESTION What was life like in Ancient Egypt?

_____

_____

_____

_____

My story

3 🛡 Look at the pictures and write a story about a boy called Abdul.

It was a hot day in Egypt. _____

_____

_____

_____

_____

_____

_____

_____

_____

_____

_____

_____

Revision 45

 **Olympic sports**

1 Complete the sports words.

1 b o x i n g
2 __ y __ __ a s t __ __ __
3 l __ __ __ j __ __ __
4 __ __ e s t l __ __ __

5 h __ __ __ __ j __ __ __
6 w e i __ __ __ l i f t __ __ __
7 f __ c __ __ __
8 r __ w __ __ __

9 h __ __ d __ __ __
10 __ __ c h __ __ __

2 Write the words from Activity 1 under the pictures.

fencing

3 Year 6 tried different sports for the first time. Which sport from Activity 2 is each student writing about?

Year 6 'TRY A NEW SPORT' DAY!

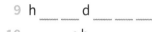
Castle Park

1 ___gymnastics___ I fell off, but, luckily, I didn't hurt myself. (Gemma)

2 _____ It was really difficult and my arrows kept missing the targets. (Taylor)

3 _____ It was great! It was like sword fighting with my brother, but with real swords. (Sam)

4 _____ I could only do 10 kg. My arms aren't very strong. (Rylan)

5 _____ I was terrible at it. I'm OK at long jump and I can jump quite high, but I can't run and jump at the same time! (Jodie)

6 _____ I fell in and got really wet! (Alice)

1 Read and match.

Language focus

1 We could play some volleyball, but I —   I'm not so good.

2 You could try to teach me,   looking in the wood.

3 We could try some archery, but   don't know how to play.

4 We could spend the next few weeks   but it could take all day.

2 Order the words to make sentences.

1 go / watch / fencing / could / I / and / the

I could go and watch the fencing .

2 you / buy / T-shirt / Mia / could / a / her / for / birthday

.

3 film / about / they / watch / could / the / tonight / Tutankhamun

.

4 put / bed / your / we / next / window / could / to / the

.

5 try / in / you / holidays / archery / could / the

.

6 party / a / we / Dad / have / could / surprise / for

.

3 Complete the dialogues using *could*.

A What do you want to do?

B We *could go snorkelling* .

A What shall we do?

B We .

A It's too far to swim.

B We .

A Any ideas?

B We .

A Oh no! My racket!

B We .

A What shall we do?

B We .

1 Complete the dialogue with the phrases from the box.

> don't think so   Why not   That's not such a good idea
> Sorry, but   ~~Why would I want to do that~~

Mia   Let's have a game of badminton.

Josh   (1) _Why would I want to do that_ ?

Mia   Because it's fun.

Josh   No, I (2) _____ .

Mia   Well, let's play football then.

Josh   (3) _____ . My mum and dad don't allow it.

Mia   (4) _____ ?

Josh   Because they say that football is bad for the grass.

Mia   We could play computer games then.

Josh   (5) _____ I haven't got a computer.

Mia   OK, then let's go to my place.

2 🎧 014 Listen and say the words.

funny   yellow
pyramid   sky

Phonics tip

There are four ways of pronouncing the letter *y*.

A funny yellow pyramid in the sky

3 Read the text. Say the words with an underlined *y* and write them in the correct sound column.

~~Jenny~~ and ~~Sylvia~~ are at ~~my~~ school. They're ~~young~~ gymnasts who hope to compete at the next Olympics. Yesterday, the girls cycled around the city park and then went to the gym. On their way home, the girls were surprised to see a huge, yellow pyramid flying slowly in the sky. 'It's a balloon … on an ice cream van!' said Sylvia. 'Why don't we get a yoghurt ice cream?' said Jenny. 'I've got some money. We've trained really hard and we haven't had a treat yet!'

yes	try	funny	symbol
young	my	Jenny	Sylvia

4 🎧 015 Listen, check and say the words.

4

1 Complete the sentences with the correct form of the words.

Language focus

I (1) **'m running** _____ (run) in the morning
With my best friend Mike.
And on Friday afternoon,
I (2) _____ (cycle) on my bike.

Then on Friday evening,
I (3) _____ (row) here with Ted.
And after that, all tired out,
I (4) _____ (go) to go to bed.

2 Write about the week of Heile Dejene, an Ethiopian marathon runner.

Monday	p.m. fly – New York	**Friday**	a.m. have TV interview
Tuesday	p.m. meet trainer		p.m. visit museum
Wednesday	p.m. run 30 km	**Saturday**	a.m. see doctor
Thursday	p.m. run 42 km		p.m. rest
		Sunday	run marathon

On Monday afternoon, Heile's flying to New York.

_____
_____
_____
_____
_____
_____
_____

3 Write four sentences about your plans for the weekend.

| B | I | U | | | | ≡ ≡ ≡ ≡ |

On Saturday morning, _____.
On Saturday afternoon, _____.
On Sunday morning, _____.
On Sunday afternoon, _____.

1 Remember the story. Complete the sentences with the correct names. Match them with the sports in the photos.

1 _____ gets a black eye. ☐

2 _____ hurts a foot. ☐

3 _____ gets wet. ☐

2 Read and order.

☐ atmosphere is amazing and they are really

☐ Patrick's foot. Finally, the children go to see the

☐ enjoying the game when Phoebe gets hit

☐ rowing, which is on a beautiful lake. Again,

☐ black eye, one has a very sore foot, and the other is soaking wet!

1 First, the children go to see a volleyball match. The

☐ that he falls in the water with a big splash. When

☐ in the face by a ball. Next, they go to a wrestling match. They have great seats

☐ the gate appears, the three children walk into it: one has a

☐ the wrestlers throws the other one through the air and he lands on

☐ the children have seats at the front. Alex gets so excited

☐ at the front. They watch a really exciting fight, but after the break, one of

3 Answer the questions with *volleyball, wrestling* or *rowing*.

At which event ...

1 does Patrick think they'll be safe?   wrestling

2 do the crowd count?   _____

3 does Phoebe get really excited?   _____

4 do they watch 32 people taking part?   _____

5 is Patrick sure about who will win?   _____

6 do the fans sing?   _____

4   **What message can we learn from the story in the Student's Book?**
Underline the best value statement.

a Watching sport is more dangerous than doing sport.

b Sport helps to bring people together.

c You should always sit down when you watch sport.

5 **Paulo, Claudia and Marcelo are three Brazilian students who want to see different Olympic sports. Read and write P (Paulo), C (Claudia) or M (Marcelo) next to each sport in the chart.**

• Paulo's favourite sports are played in or on water, but he doesn't mind ball games.

• Claudia doesn't like sports which involve fighting or weapons. She likes athletics and gymnastics.

• Marcelo loves sports that involve fighting and weapons. He doesn't enjoy athletics.

TODAY'S EVENTS			
10 a.m.–12 p.m.	rowing [P]	wrestling [ ]	gymnastics [ ]
1 p.m.–3 p.m.	long jump [ ]	swimming [ ]	archery [ ]
3 p.m.–5 p.m.	boxing [ ]	high jump [ ]	diving [ ]
5 p.m.–7 p.m.	football [ ]	hurdles [ ]	fencing [ ]

6 **Read the sentences and look at the timetable in Activity 5.**
Tick ✓ the true sentences and correct the sports in the false sentences.

1 Claudia is watching some ~~athletics~~ from 10 a.m. to 12 p.m.   _gymnastics_

2 Marcelo is watching the archery from 1 p.m. to 3 p.m.   _____

3 Paulo is watching the long jump from 1 p.m. to 3 p.m.   _____

4 Claudia is watching the diving after the long jump.   _____

5 Paulo is watching the football after the diving.   _____

6 Marcelo is watching the boxing before the hurdles.   _____

7 **Plan your perfect day at the Olympics. Choose any sports that you know in English.**

Next Monday at the Olympics:

10 a.m.–12 p.m. I'm watching the _____ . 3 p.m.–5 p.m. _____

1 p.m.–3 p.m. _____   5 p.m.–7 p.m. _____

1 🎧 016 Listen to Maxine talking to Adam about a sports afternoon. What sport did each person do? Write a letter (A–H) next to each person. There is one example.

People

1 Ellie ☐
2 Justin ☐
3 Stacey ☐
4 Adam ☐ F
5 James ☐

Sport

A
B
C
D
E
F
G
H

2 🎧 017 Listen again and answer the questions.

1 Who told Maxine that Adam liked sports? Her brother.
2 When was the sports afternoon? _____ .
3 Why didn't Maxine go? _____ .
4 Why couldn't Adam try fencing? _____ .
5 Why couldn't Justin play tennis? _____ .
6 What is Adam going to try next week? _____ .

3 Complete the five conversations. Choose A, B or C.

1 I don't want to go to the wrestling match.

   A Yes, I like it too.   B Why did you watch it?   Ⓒ Let's not go then.

2 Is there time before the game starts?

   A Yes, about half an hour.   B That's all right.   C You're welcome.

3 I'm sorry, there aren't any tickets left.

   A It would be great.   B What a pity!   C I hope so.

4 What are you going to see tomorrow morning?

   A At 11 o'clock.   B I saw the high jump.   C The long jump.

5 See you in half an hour.

   A No, I'm not.   B Don't be late.   C I don't see.

1 Look and read. Write 1, 2, 3 or 4 words to complete the sentences about the email.

Hi,

It was great to get your email. Thanks for writing. We had a great time on our school trip last week. We went with our P.E. (that's Physical Education) teacher, Mr Bennett, to visit the Olympic Park in London. We went on a bus to London, then we went on the London Underground.

The first thing we did when we arrived was have our lunch. We took packed lunches, so we ate our sandwiches outdoors next to some amazing fountains. One of the boys didn't listen to Mr Bennett, and he went too close to one of the fountains. It started suddenly and he got really wet!

The best part of the trip was when we had a tour of the Olympic Stadium. We saw the athletes' changing rooms and we even ran on their warm-up track. It's amazing to think I've run on the same track as Usain Bolt!

I'd like to ask you a few questions about sport. What sports do you play at your school? What's the most popular sport for girls? What's the most popular sport for boys? What other things do you and your friends like doing in your free time? Please send me a photo of you doing a sport.

Write soon!

Sophia

1 Sophia's class went to London by _____ bus _____ .
2 _____ is Sophia's P.E. teacher.
3 The children had _____ for lunch.
4 They ate their lunch _____ some fountains.
5 One boy went _____ of the fountains!
6 The tour of the stadium was the _____ of the trip.
7 Sophia _____ the athletes' warm-up track.

2 Write Sophia an email. Answer the questions. Write 25–35 words.

Think and learn

1 **Look and match.**

weightlifter · boxer · gymnast · rower · fencer · long jumper

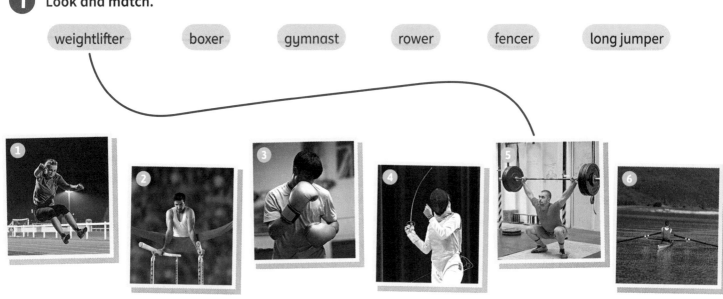

2 **Who uses it? Look and write words from Activity 1.**

¹w e i ²g h t l i ³f t e r

3 **Complete the sentences.**

balance   speed   ~~stamina~~   strength   lower body   upper body

1 If you want to run 20 km, you need to build up your ___stamina___ .

2 I'm doing these arm exercises to make my _____ stronger.

3 You need a lot of _____ to lift heavy weights.

4 Gymnasts need good _____ to stay on the narrow equipment.

5 If she wants to win races, she'll need to improve her _____ .

6 Long jumpers and high jumpers need to have a very strong _____ .

4 Read and write *t* (true), *f* (false) or *ds* (doesn't say).

WHAT CAN WE LEARN FROM OLYMPIC ATHLETES?

You might want to run a kilometre or win the long jump on Sports Day, but how do Olympic athletes train to win a gold medal? Some of the answers might surprise you.

Of course, it's important to be good at your sport and to practise it often, but it's also good to try some different exercises too. Runners sometimes swim or cycle to improve their stamina. Fencers might do some work on the running track to improve their speed and wrestlers can spend a lot of time weightlifting to build up their strength.

It's important to rest your body too. Top athletes have at least one day each week when they take a break from training, so their bodies can recover.

As well as having a break from exercise, athletes need to get a lot of sleep. Olympic athletes often sleep for ten hours a night and many of them are in bed by 9 o'clock!

Eating the right food is very important too. Athletes need the right balance of food to give them energy and keep them healthy. Carbohydrates are great for energy, but they also need a lot of protein, fruit and vegetables. Of course, they need to drink plenty of water too.

1 You need to focus on just one sport if you want to do well. _____f_____

2 Swimming and cycling can help build up stamina. _____

3 Running can improve your strength. _____

4 Top athletes train every day of the week. _____

5 Olympic athletes have to get up early every day. _____

6 Athletes need to eat a variety of different food types. _____

5 ⭐ Project 🛡️ **What exercises do they need to do? Read and match.**

 **1** ~~I need to build stamina.~~

2 I need to build strength.

3 I need to build speed.

4 I need to improve my balance.

 a

 b

 c

 d [1]

1 Choose six words or phrases to complete the sentences.

> She could   They're flying   am visiting   ~~could go~~   We're going
>
> could we   are flying   could   visiting my   having a

1 We _____could go_____ and see a film later.

2 I'm _____ aunt this weekend.

3 _____ buy her dad a book for his birthday.

4 _____ rowing on Saturday.

5 He's _____ piano lesson tomorrow.

6 _____ to Greece in the morning.

2 Join the parts to make words and use them to complete the sentences.

> row   climb   ~~fen~~   bal   hur   stam
>
> ina   dles   ance   ing   ing   ~~cing~~

1 I think _____fencing_____ is dangerous. Those swords are really sharp.

2 They were _____ across the lake when their boat sank.

3 The gymnast's _____ was amazing – she didn't fall once.

4 We were watching the _____ when one of the athletes fell over.

5 If you are scared of heights, you won't like _____.

6 You need a lot of _____ to run a long race.

3 Complete the sentences with your own ideas.

1 We could _____ this evening.

2 I'm _____ at 10 a.m. next Saturday.

3 We're _____ tonight.

4 My mum's _____ on Monday evening.

5 We could _____ for lunch.

6 He's _____ tomorrow morning.

What do I know?

1 Read and tick ☑. Then write examples.

1 I can use *could* for possibility. ☐

'Any ideas?' '_____ ,'

'What shall we do?' '_____ ,'

2 I can use the present continuous to talk about the future. ☐

_____

_____

3 I can write the names of five Olympic sports. ☐

_____ _____ _____

_____ _____

2 🛡 Write sentences to answer the Big Question.

BIG QUESTION What do we know about sports?

_____
_____
_____
_____

My weekend

3 🛡 Imagine you are planning your weekend with a friend. Write a dialogue. Use the ideas to help you.

- Suggest doing something at a certain time.
- Your friend has other plans for that time.
- Make another suggestion.
- Your friend isn't interested in that activity.
- Make one more suggestion.
- Your friend agrees to the plan.

A: Let's _____
_____
_____
_____
_____
_____
_____
_____
_____
_____

5 In London

1 Complete the shops and match them with the photos.

1 **b** a k e **r** 's

2 ___ r o ___ ___ ___ 's

3 ___ ___ ___ c h ___ ___ 's

4 ___ a ___ b ___ ___ 's

5 ___ e w ___ ___ ___ e ___ 's

6 ___ ___ ___ p ___ t ___ ___ ___ 's

7 ___ h ___ m ___ ___ ___ 's

8 ___ a i ___ o ___ 's

2 Which of the shops from Activity 1 are these people in?

1 'Would you like some chicken?' _____butcher's_____

2 'Have you got any toothpaste?' _____

3 'How much is it for a hair wash?' _____

4 'I want a special necklace for my wife's birthday.' _____

5 'These trousers are too long.' _____

6 'Can you make me some chairs too?' _____

7 'I'd like some apples, please.' _____

8 'How much is that cake?' _____

3 Complete the email with the words from the box.

> interesting   wood   people   built   buildings   ~~finished~~   Thames

Hi Carlos,

You asked me for some information for your project. Well, yesterday I (1) _____finished_____ reading a book about The Great Fire of London. It was quite (2) _____. At that time, only about 200,000 (3) _____ lived in London. Today, there are eight million. Anyway, in September 1666, a fire started north of the River (4) _____ and the city burned for four days. Almost 80% of the (5) _____ were destroyed. After the fire, London was (6) _____ again with wider streets and houses made of brick, not (7) _____.

Write and tell me if you need more information. We don't study Spanish history – only Spanish words!

Dylan

1 Read and circle the correct words.

Have you (1) ever / never been to London Zoo?
You've got family there.
Yes, I (2) **have** / **am**. I saw my cousins.
They live next to the bear.

Has she (3) **ever** / **never** been to London Zoo?
Monkeys live there too.
No, she (4) **hasn't** / **doesn't**. She's (5) **ever** / **never** been.
She doesn't like the zoo!

2 Match the past participles from the box with the correct verbs.

caught   ~~seen~~   sung   eaten   been   found   drunk   won   slept   broken   ridden   driven

1 see – _____seen_____
2 win – _____
3 ride – _____
4 sing – _____

5 eat – _____
6 drive – _____
7 be – _____
8 find – _____

9 sleep – _____
10 drink – _____
11 break – _____
12 catch – _____

3 Complete the dialogues. Use *ever* and *never*.

1 A _____Have you ever baked_____ bread? (bake)
   B No, _I've never baked_ bread, but I _'ve baked_____ cakes with my dad. (bake)

2 A _____ a monster? (see)
   B No, _____ a monster, but I _____ people in costumes! (see)

3 A _____ crocodile eggs? (eat)
   B No, _____ crocodile eggs, but I _____ lots of hen's eggs. (eat)

4 A _____ your leg? (break)
   B No, _____ my leg, but I _____ my arm. (break)

4 Look at the pictures. Write questions and answers.

1 A _Has he ever been to Mexico?_____   B _No, he hasn't, but he's been to Colombia._
2 A _____   B _____
3 A _____   B _____
4 A _____   B _____

1 🎧 **018** Listen and match the rhyming words. Write two more words for each rhyme.

1 street ——— there _____ _____
2 home   do _____ _____
3 square ——— meet ——— feet _____
4 zoo   own _____ _____

2 🎮 Remember the song. Write questions asking about each city. Then answer them.

1 Have you ever been
_____ ?
_____

2 _____
_____ ?
_____

3 _____
_____ ?
_____

3 🎧 **019** Listen and say the sentence.

**Snakes hi<u>ss</u> and
bees bu<u>zz</u>.**

Phonics tip

Make an *sss* sound like a snake
and a *zzz* sound like a bee.
Can you hear the difference?

4 Say the words from the box and write them in the correct sound column.

<del>thi<u>s</u></del> i<u>s</u> ama<u>z</u>ing <u>s</u>o
animal<u>s</u> <u>c</u>ity li<u>s</u>ten
reali<u>s</u>e shark<u>s</u> paint<u>s</u>
pre<u>s</u>ent eye<u>s</u> con<u>c</u>ert
noi<u>s</u>e e<u>s</u>cape<u>s</u> bridge<u>s</u>

Sam		Zara	
this		is	

5 🎧 **020** Listen, check and say the words.

1 Read and circle the correct words.

Language focus

Have you ever (1) (seen) / see the sea?   I (3) **have** / **had** a swim and then

Yes, I (2) **have**, / **had**, in May.   I (4) **go** / **went** home straightaway.

2 Match the questions with the answers.

1 Have you ever tried coconut milk? [d]

2 Have your parents ever been to the UK? [ ]

3 Has your brother ever read a
Harry Potter book? [ ]

4 Have you ever seen a Shakespeare play? [ ]

5 Have I ever played badminton? [ ]

6 Have you ever found any money? [ ]

a Yes, they have. They were in London in March.

b Yes, I have. I saw *Romeo and Juliet* with my
grandparents last summer.

c Yes, you have. We played it on the beach last
year. Remember?

d ~~Yes, I have. I tried it last year in Brazil.~~

e No, I haven't, but I found a key in the street
last year.

f No, he hasn't, but he watched all the films
last month.

3 Look at the photos and write dialogues.

1 last winter

2 on holiday

3

4 in the summer

5 in July

last month

1 A Have you ever been skiing? B Yes, I have. I went last winter.

2 A _____ B _____

3 A _____ B _____

4 A _____ B _____

5 A _____ B _____

1 🛡 Remember the story. Tick ✓ the form of transport which is not in the story.

① ☐   ② ☐   ③ ☐   ④ ☐

2 🛡 Match the information (a–e) with the gaps (1–8) in the summary.

a Patrick rescues the boy

b to leave the city

c Mr Fisher is worried

d from a raft onto a boat

e but there isn't enough room for everyone

f ~~where his wife and children are waiting~~

g put a big chest onto the cart

h who are trying to escape across the river

The children go with Mr Fisher and he tells them about the fire. He invites the children to escape with his family to the countryside and he takes them to his house, (1) ☐ f . On the way there, they see lots of people (2) ☐ in boats. They see a man step (3) ☐ and a child falls into the water. (4) ☐ and the woman on the boat gives him a bracelet to say thank you.

They arrive at Mr Fisher's house and help him (5) ☐. Then they all get onto it (6) ☐, but just then a woman arrives with a group of children. She wants to go with them, (7) ☐. The friends jump down from the cart and give their spaces to the woman and the children. (8) ☐, but they tell him that they know another way to escape and they leave through the gate.

3 🛡 Complete the puzzle. Look at the shaded boxes and find the name of the king of England at the time of The Great Fire.

1 Some people took these animals onto the boats with them.

2 The people were trying to cross this river.

3 This is flat, made of wood and you can travel on water with it.

4 Mr Fisher has two of these animals.

5 A woman gives this to Patrick.

6 This is a word for chairs, armchairs, sofas and tables.

7 This is a big box.

The king at the time of The Great Fire of London was King _____ II.

4 Read about the man trying to escape from The Great Fire. Can you help him?

A man is trying to escape by boat across the River Thames. He wants to take his pet fox, his chicken and a bag of grain with him. His boat is small, so he can only take one thing with him each time. If he leaves the chicken and the grain together, the chicken will eat the grain. If he leaves the fox and the chicken together, the fox will eat the chicken. How can he get all three things safely to the other side?

He should ...

_____

_____ .

5 Look at the pictures. How could the children show that they are thinking of others? Complete the sentences.

He could *give her his seat* .

She could _____ .

He could _____ .

She could _____ .

6 Tick ✔ the best thing to say for each picture in Activity 5.

1 a Sit here. ☐

  b Would you like this seat? ✔

2 a Those bags look heavy. ☐

  b Can I help you with those? ☐

3 a Shall I reach that for you? ☐

  b You're too short. ☐

4 a You've dropped some money. ☐

  b I'll get that for you. ☐

1 Look at the photos. Complete the texts with the names of the places.

The Tower of London

Covent Garden

The Natural History Museum

a
About 100 years ago, (1) _____Covent Garden_____ was a busy fruit and vegetable market. Over the years, it has changed a lot and now it is a very popular tourist destination. There are many small independent shops and you can find lots of interesting things to buy.

b
If you're interested in the story of life on Earth, a trip to London isn't complete without a visit to the (2) _____, which contains over 80 million items.

c
Visitors from all over the world come to see the (3) _____, the large stone building next to London Bridge. It is nearly 1,000 years old. In the past, it has been a palace, a castle and a prison.

d
The exhibits in the (4) _____ cover 4.5 billion years of the Earth's history. It is most famous for its dinosaurs, but you can also see an enormous blue whale skeleton, lots of fossils, and a piece of rock from Mars.

e
A lot of kings and queens have lived in the (5) _____. At one time, all the money in Britain was made here. Today, the Crown Jewels, a collection of the king's or queen's very precious jewels, is kept here.

f
(6) _____ is now famous for entertainment. It is the home of the Royal Opera House, the most famous place to see opera in the UK.

g
There are many stories and legends about the (7) _____. Some people say they have seen ghosts there. Others say that if the black birds that live there fly away, it will fall down!

h
If you don't like opera music, or if it's too expensive, you can just sit and watch one of the many street performers in (8) _____ for free.

i
You have to pay for some exhibitions in the (9) _____, but there are plenty of things to see for free. Sometimes, you can even visit at nighttime!

1 (021) You will hear a woman asking for information about a train. Listen and complete the notes.

Train

To: (1) London

Day of journey: (2) _____

Train leaves at: (3) _____

Return ticket costs: (4) _____

Food on train: (5) Drinks and _____

Website address: (6) _____

2 Alison wants to go to London on Thursday. She needs to get there by 10 a.m. She phones for some information. Write a dialogue.

Alison: Hello. I'd like some information about trains to London, please.

Man: _____

_____

_____

_____

_____

_____

_____

3 Read the sentences about a trip to London. Choose the best word (A, B or C) for each space.

1 Lucy and Julia … on a school trip to London last week.

(A) went   B visited   C came

2 The first … that they visited was the Tower of London.

A museum   B place   C market

3 They … lots of photos with their phones.

A made   B did   C took

4 The teacher then took the children on a guided … of the Tower.

A visit   B tour   C walk

5 Lucy and Julia got lost and walked … the wrong corridor.

A in   B over   C down

6 They opened a door and … a ghost!

A spoke   B talk   C met

1 **Read and match.**

1 A cone   is perfectly round, like a ball.

2 A cube   has two circular ends and curved sides.

3 A cuboid   has six sides, all squares.

4 A cylinder   has six sides, which can be squares or rectangles.

5 A pyramid   has a circular bottom and sides which meet at a point.

6 A sphere   has a square bottom and sides which are shaped like triangles.

2 **Look, read and write. Which shape from Activity 1 are these buildings most like?**

SHAPES ALL AROUND US

We've already looked at the shapes of some buildings in London, but have you ever seen these ones?

1 The Copper Box Arena was built for the 2012 Olympic Games. Handball and fencing events were held there. Its name describes it perfectly, as it's a _____cuboid_____ made from copper.

2 Some buildings even include a shape in their name. This modern art gallery is exactly that – a white _____, with a glass roof and narrow windows.

3 Another art gallery with a distinctively shaped building is the Tate Modern. The main building opened in 2000, but in 2016 a new part opened, called the _____ Tower.

4 There aren't many buildings shaped like _____s in London, but there are plans to build one in East London, for concerts and sports events. The ones in the picture are in Cornwall.

5 Construction can happen below the ground as well as above, and we can see 3D shapes there too. This London Underground train runs through a tunnel in the shape of a _____.

The Copper Box Arena

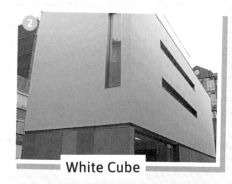

White Cube

The Tate Modern

The London Underground

The Eden Project

3 Look at the photos. What is similar about all the houses?

All the houses _____.

WHAT IS THE BEST SHAPE FOR A HOUSE?

In the past, houses in many cultures were round. Igloos, tepees, yurts and some stone or mud round houses are all based on the shape of a cylinder or sphere. At some point, builders started to build more cuboid houses. Perhaps it was easier to split bigger houses into rooms when they were this shape, or maybe more houses could be packed into a smaller space if they had straight sides. No-one is certain why this change happened. Today, however, many architects think that there are advantages to building houses in the shape of cylinders:

• They take less time to build and use fewer materials.
• They are stronger than a shape with several sides.
• They are warmer because they need less energy to heat them.
• They are very safe in strong winds because the wind blows round them.
• They are quieter because sound also flows round them, rather than crashing into them.

Perhaps this is the future of housing. What do you think?

4 Read the article in Activity 3 and write *t* (true), *f* (false) or *ds* (doesn't say).

1 Building round houses is a new idea. _f_
2 People started building cuboid houses because they were cheaper. ____
3 It is quicker to build a round house than a cuboid house. ____
4 Round houses can blow down easily in a storm. ____
5 It isn't as noisy inside a round house. ____
6 Round houses are more popular than cuboid houses now. ____

5 Project — Choose a shape and find out about a famous building that is built in that shape. Draw it. Answer these questions:

• What is it called?
• Where is it?
• Who designed it?
• When was it built?
• What is it made from?
• What is it used for?

The Louvre Pyramid, Paris

It was designed by I.M. Pei, a Chinese architect, and built in 1989. The pyramid is made of metal and glass. It is the main entrance to the Louvre Museum.

1 Draw lines and complete the sentences with the words from the box.

ever been   TV last   ~~any money~~   lost my   never watched a   last year

1 Have you ever	football match	in the street?
2 Has she	the film on	her mum _____.
3 I have _____	_____ to	_____ night.
4 I didn't like	pen at	on TV!
5 She went	found _any money_	school yesterday.
6 I _____	to Spain with	a foreign country?

2 Find the words and use them to complete the sentences.

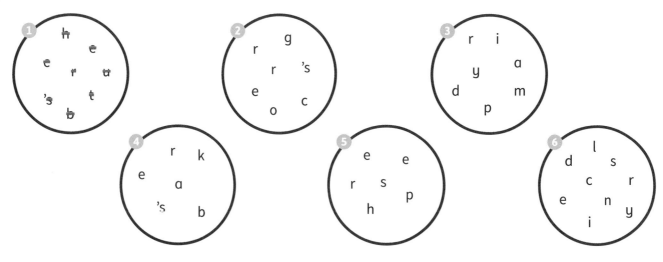

1 There's really good meat at our local _____ butcher's _____.
2 We get all our vegetables at our local _____.
3 A cone and a _____ are similar, but a cone has a round bottom.
4 I love the smell of fresh bread coming from the _____.
5 A _____ is another name for a ball shape.
6 Lots of tunnels are shaped like _____ because they are very strong.

3 Complete the sentences with your own ideas.

1 Have you ever _____?
2 I've never _____.
3 I _____ last night.
4 Have _____ Japanese food?
5 We _____ in 2015.
6 Has she ever _____?

What do I know?

1 Read and tick ✓. Then write examples.

1 I can use the present perfect with *ever* and *never*. ☐

_____

_____

2 I can use the past simple to give detail with the present perfect. ☐

_____

_____

3 I can write the names of five shops. ☐

_____ _____ _____

_____ _____

2 🛡 Write sentences to answer the Big Question.

BIG QUESTION Why is London famous?

_____

_____

_____

_____

My story

3 🛡 Look at the pictures and write the story.

Mario was a chef. _____

_____

_____

_____

_____

_____

_____.

1 Find ten more words about tools and machines in the word search.

h	s	c	r	e	w	d	r	i	v	e	r
a	s	w	o	r	k	b	e	n	c	h	s
m	h	p	a	b	u	t	t	o	n	y	a
m	d	r	i	l	l	n	a	i	l	s	w
e	p	a	i	n	t	b	r	u	s	h	f
r	s	p	a	n	n	e	r	l	g	r	t
s	w	i	t	c	h	l	e	v	e	r	n

Which word from Student's Book page 70 is missing?

_____

2 Match the words from Activity 1 with the pictures.

1 _____workbench_____
2 _____
3 _____
4 _____
5 _____
6 _____
7 _____
8 _____
9 _____
10 _____
11 _____
12 _____

3 Choose words from Activity 2 to complete the dialogue.

Phoebe   Well, he certainly looks like a professor. Let's go over to his (1) _____workbench_____ and talk to him.

Patrick   Excuse me.

Professor   Just a minute. Just a minute. I've nearly finished. Pass me that (2) _____, please, and a few (3) _____.

Alex   Here you are.

Professor   Thank you … Now one quick turn of the (4) _____ and that's it!

1 Complete with *too many* or *not enough*.

I've got (1) _____too many_____ jobs to do.

I have (2) _____ got _____ time.

I think I need to go and see

A very good friend of mine!

It's got (3) _____ buttons

And (4) _____ power.

To clean this mess, it's going to take

A lot more than an hour.

2 Read and circle the correct words.

1 Sorry, I can't help you with your homework. I haven't got **too many** / (**enough**) time.

2 You can't have a high mark because there are **too many** / **not enough** mistakes in your test.

3 I'm so busy. I've got **too many** / **not enough** things to do.

4 We can't have some food first. There's **too many** / **not enough** time before the train leaves.

5 I don't like driving here. There are **too many** / **not enough** holes in the road.

6 I can't buy the shirt today because I haven't got **too many** / **enough** money.

3 Complete the dialogue with *too many* and *not enough*.

Paul   We have (1) _n't_ got _enough_ food for the party.

Lily   Yes, we have. Last time we made (2) _____ sandwiches and we were eating them all weekend!

Eva   But there is (3) _____ to drink – we only have one carton of orange juice.

Paul   OK, I'll get some more orange juice.

Eva   There are (4) _____ chairs in the room. We need more space to dance.

4 Look at the pictures. Write sentences with *too many* or *not enough*.

1 _There isn't enough food._   2 _____   3 _____

4 _____   5 _____   6 _____ on Team B.

1 🔲 **Read the dialogue in the Student's Book again. Complete the summary.**

Lucy's (1) _____hobby_____ is inventing things. She says she's making a (2) _____ to get rid of her (3) _____! It's very (4) _____ and (5) _____ to understand.

2 **Complete the dialogue with the phrases from the box.**

> reason is that   Why not   That's because   That's why   ~~finished it yet~~   what's it for

Max   Hey, what are you doing?

Mia   I'm making a machine for my Science project, but I haven't (1) __finished it yet.__

Max   Where's the machine? It looks to me like you're just eating strawberries!

Mia   Ah! (2) _____ it's part of my research.

Max   OK ... so where's the machine? And (3) _____?

Mia   Well, it brings snacks to me. But I can't show you yet.

Max   (4) _____?

Mia   Because I need to do more research. (5) _____ I'm eating strawberries.

Max   So, the (6) _____ you need to eat more strawberries?

Mia   Yes, exactly. So ... could you bring me some, please?

3 🎧 022 **Listen and say the words.**

light   enough   through

Phonics tip

There are different ways of pronouncing the letters *gh*.

88 kg

88 kg

Mighty Mike

A weightlifter

4 **Match the rhyming words.**

1	high	c		a	graph
2	laugh			b	stuff
3	through			c	~~fly~~
4	caught			d	zoo
5	enough			e	bought

6	light			f	plate
7	eight			g	show
8	thought			h	white
9	cough			i	short
10	although			j	off

5 🎧 023 **Listen, check and say the words.**

1 Put the words in order to make questions.

1 machine / you / is / tell / Can / me / the / what / ?

_____

2 does / me / Can / button / tell / what / you / this / ?

_____

3 me / machine / for / tell / the / Can / is / you / what / ?

_____

2 Read and order the dialogue.

[ ] Bradley   The green button?

[ ] Bradley   Ah, to cook them. And can you tell me what this switch is for?

[1] Bradley   Can you tell me what this machine is?

[ ] Bradley   Mmm, I like soup. Can you tell me what this lever does?

[ ] Bradley   I love your machine. Can I try some soup now?

[ ] Professor When you press that lever, all the vegetables fall into hot water.

[ ] Professor Yes, when you press the green button, the soup is put into cans and you can drink it.

[ ] Professor Certainly. It makes lots of different vegetable soups.

[ ] Professor Certainly. Here you are.

[ ] Professor It's for starting the knives inside. They cut up all the vegetables. Finally, you press the green button.

3 Look at the pictures. Write questions with *is*, *does* and *is for*. Answer them with your own ideas.

1 A Can you tell me what this button does? B Yes, it opens the parachute.

2 A _____ B _____

3 A _____ B _____

4 A _____ B _____

1 🛡 **Remember the story. Read and match.**

1 The painting machine | d | a should change how people look.

2 The Homework Express | | b should move things about the room.

3 The tele-transporter | | c should answer questions.

4 The hairdressing machine | | d ~~should change the colour of things~~.

2 🛡 **Look at the photos. Complete the summary with the words for five of the objects.**

The professor shows the children his painting machine. He asks them to choose a colour for the chair. They choose red and yellow spots. The professor pushes a (1) _____switch_____ and the (2) _____ on the machine paint the cat green and blue instead. Next, he shows them the Homework Express. He asks them to choose a subject, so they pick Maths and they give the professor a sum. He types it into the machine and the answer 'Paris' appears.

The next machine which he shows them is the tele-transporter. You put an object in it, press a (3) _____ and the object appears on the other side of the room. Unfortunately, his experiment with a bike doesn't work and he'll need to use his (4) _____. Finally, he shows them a hairdressing machine, but Phoebe doesn't want to try it out. Patrick asks him about another machine. The professor tells him not to touch it, but it's too late. Patrick pulls the (5) _____ and the gate appears.

3 **Complete the sentences with the correct name.**

1 _____Phoebe_____ chooses the colours for the chair.

2 _____ asks about the Homework Express.

3 _____ chooses the sum for the Homework Express.

4 _____ needs a tool.

5 _____ wants Phoebe to try the hairdressing machine.

4 Here are some wrong answers from the Homework Express. Match each answer with the question it was trying to answer.

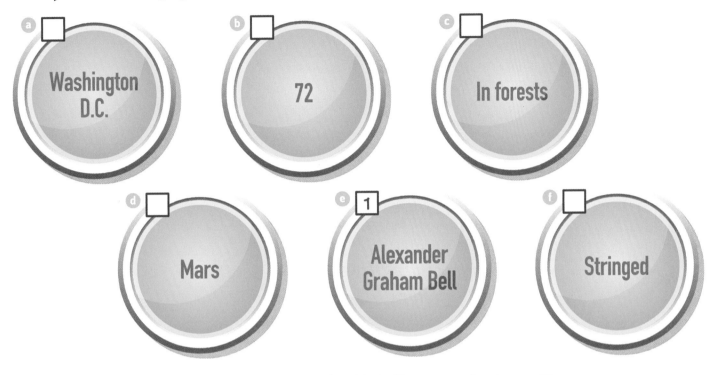

a ☐ Washington D.C.

b ☐ 72

c ☐ In forests

d ☐ Mars

e ☐ 1 Alexander Graham Bell

f ☐ Stringed

1 Who invented the plane?

4 What kind of instrument is a trumpet?

2 What is 9 x 9?

5 Where do sharks live?

3 What is the capital of Italy?

6 What's the biggest planet in the solar system?

5 The answers from the Homework Express in Activity 4 are all wrong. Write the correct answers.

1 Alberto Santos-Dumont _____

2 _____

3 _____

4 _____

5 _____

6 _____

6 Look at the machine's wrong answers in Activity 4. Write the correct questions.

a What is the capital of the USA? _____

b _____

c _____

d _____

e _____

f _____

1 What message can we learn from the webpage in the Student's Book? <u>Underline</u> the best value statement.

a The most important inventions help people.

b The most important inventions are expensive.

c The most expensive inventions help people.

2 Look and read. Write the correct word for each description. Not all the words are used.

spanner   switch   lever   drill

television

1 This is for cutting wood.   saw
2 You can walk and talk with one of these.   _____
3 Many children like watching this.   _____
4 You can make holes in walls with this.   _____
5 When you turn on a light, you use this.   _____
6 This has made it easier to travel round the world. _____

plane

radio   saw   car   mobile phone

3 Read about two early inventions and write *t* (true), *f* (false) or *ds* (doesn't say).

FIRE

Was fire invented or discovered? Fire wasn't really invented – it existed without humans. But when early humans invented ways of controlling fire and making it themselves, it changed the way they lived. They could stay warm, protect themselves and, perhaps most importantly, cook food. No-one is certain when humans first started using fire, but it was somewhere between two million and 125,000 years ago.

THE WHEEL

The earliest examples of the wheel come from around 5,500 years ago. They were from an area at the eastern end of the Mediterranean Sea, then called Mesopotamia. They were wooden and they were used to make pots. Wheeled vehicles came along a few hundred years later, when people worked out how to fix wheels to carts or chariots. The wheel is such an amazing invention because it isn't related to anything in nature.

1 People learned to cook food before the wheel was invented.   t

2 Early humans started using fire over two million years ago.   _____

3 Before they could control fire, humans were always cold.   _____

4 Wheels weren't used for transport at first.   _____

5 Today, most of Mesopotamia is in Iraq.   _____

6 The wheel is based on something you can see in nature.   _____

1 **024** You will hear some information about a museum. Listen and complete the notes.

GREAT INVENTIONS MUSEUM

YOU CAN SEE ...

DOWNSTAIRS

Red room: (1)   _Old typewriters_
Green room: (2)   _____

UPSTAIRS

Left gallery: (3)   _____
Right gallery: More than 300 (4) _____
Price of guidebook: (5)   _____
Museum closes at: (6)   _____

2 Match the notices (A–H) with the instructions (1–6). Write the correct letter. There are two extra notices.

A PRIVATE KEEP OUT

B  Press to hear explanation

C Please do not touch

D Fire exit

E  NO FOOD OR DRINK

F HAVE YOU HANDED IN YOUR RUCKSACK?

1 If there is an emergency, go out of this door.   [D]

2 You must not make any noise at the moment.   [ ]

3 You must not carry big bags in the museum.   [ ]

4 You can't go into this room.   [ ]

5 You aren't allowed to eat here.   [ ]

6 If you touch this button, you will hear someone talking.   [ ]

G  **KEEP QUIET** Talk in progress

H ALL CHILDREN MUST BE WITH AN ADULT

Think and learn

1 Read and circle the correct words .

1 Levers help us to (**lift things**)/ **join things together**.

2 Pulleys use a wheel and a **rope** / **ramp** to move things.

3 Wheels and axles help us to move things using **circular** / **high** parts.

4 **Ramps** / **Screws** help us to move heavy things from low to high, or high to low.

5 Screws help us to **join things together** / **move things**.

6 Wedges are used to cut or separate things, or to **stop things from moving** / **lift heavy things**.

7 The **wedge** / **lever** family includes ramps and screws.

8 The **wedge** / **lever** family includes wheels and axles, and pulleys.

2 What kinds of machines are they? Look and write. You can use the words more than once.

> lever   wheel and axle   pulley   ramp   screw   wedge

screw

3 Which family are they in? Look again at the photos from Activity 2 and write the numbers in the correct place.

lever family				
wedge family	1			

78 Science

4 What are they? Look and write the letter.

a
b
c

1 rollercoaster ☐
2 fishing rod ☐
3 tin opener ☐

5 Read and write the names of the machines from Activity 4.

Simple and compound machines

A compound machine is a combination of two or more different simple machines. The different machines work together and can do more difficult jobs than simple machines can do on their own. Let's look at some of the examples around you.

1 lever
2 _____
3 _____

A _____ helps you to get into your baked beans. But can you guess what simple machines it uses? Well, it actually uses four – levers, a wheel and axle, a screw and a wedge!

4 _____

Something else that could help you with food is a _____. This compound machine consists of a lever, a wheel and axle, and a pulley.

8 _____
9 _____
6 _____
7 _____

A _____ is even more complex. It uses almost every kind of simple machine, but it's the ramps that make it so much fun!

10 _____
11 _____
12 _____

6 Read the text in Activity 5 again and label the diagrams with the names of the simple machines.

7 ⭐ Project 🛡 Find an example of a compound machine in your home. Draw it and write sentences about it.

Think about:
- what it is for and what it does.
- what simple machines it is made of.
- what the simple machines do.

_____
_____
_____

1 Correct the sentences by writing the missing words from the box in the right place.

> too   does   what   ~~enough~~   you   many

1 He didn't get sleep last night. He's really tired.

   He didn't get enough sleep last night. He's really tired.

2 Can you tell me this machine is for?

   _____?

3 She's got many posters and nowhere to put them all.

   _____.

4 Can tell me what this is?

   _____?

5 I've got too clothes. I need to give some away.

   _____.

6 Can you tell me what this switch?

   _____?

2 Join the parts to make words and use them to complete the sentences.

> inven   paint   pull   ~~but~~   le   ham

> brush   ~~ton~~   mer   ver   tion   eys

1 If you press that _____**button**_____, the machine will explode!

2 I think TV is the greatest _____ of all time. I love it!

3 Why don't you use a _____ to help you lift the sofa?

4 You can find wheels in _____, as well as in wheel and axle machines.

5 He dropped a _____ when he was up the ladder. It made a real mess!

6 She missed the nail and she hit her finger with the _____!

3 Complete the sentences with your own ideas.

1 I've got too _____.

2 I haven't got enough _____.

3 _____ does?

4 Can you tell me _____?

5 _____ too much homework.

6 _____ is for?

What do I know?

1 Read and tick ✓. Then write examples.

1 I can write sentences with *too many* and *not enough*. ☐

_____

_____

2 I can write sentences with *Can you tell me what this is / does / is for?* ☐

_____

_____

_____

3 I can write the names of five types of tool. ☐

_____ _____ _____

_____ _____

2 🛡 Write sentences to answer the Big Question.

BIG QUESTION How do inventions help us?

_____

_____

_____

_____

My bike

3 🛡 Imagine you are showing your new 'superbike' to a friend. Write a dialogue.

• Your friend asks you what the switches/buttons/levers do.

• You explain what they are, what they do or what they are for.

_____

_____

_____

_____

_____

_____

_____

_____

_____

_____

7 This is Houston

1 Look at the pictures. Complete the words.

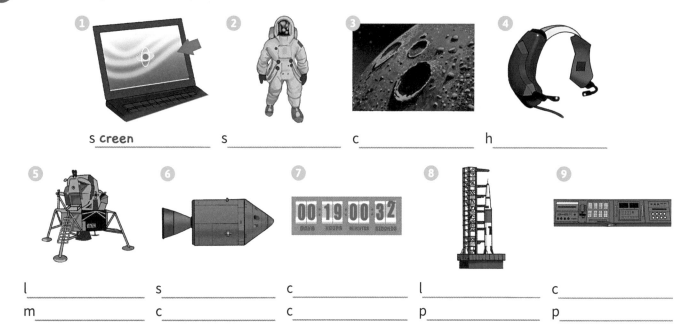

s **creen**   s _____   c _____   h _____

l _____   s _____   c _____   l _____   c _____

m _____   c _____   c _____   p _____   p _____

2 Correct one moon landing word in each sentence.

1 There was something wrong with the ~~headset~~ and the astronauts didn't know the temperature.   _control panel_

2 When the space capsule reached zero, the rocket took off.   _____

3 They couldn't speak to the astronaut because he wasn't wearing his launch pad.   _____

4 The astronauts put on their control panels and climbed into the rocket.   _____

5 The lunar module landed in a large countdown clock on the moon.   _____

6 Before they took off, the astronauts sat in the crater and checked the control panel.   _____

3 Read and match.

1 The three children have landed   [d]   a shows the Saturn V rocket.

2 The photo on the wall   [ ]   b asks them what they are doing.

3 It was taken   [ ]   c they could be spies.

4 One of the engineers   [ ]   d ~~in Houston, Texas. It is 1969.~~

5 Patrick explains that   [ ]   e they are from the future.

6 A security officer thinks that   [ ]   f four days ago.

1 Complete the sentences with the gerund of the verbs in brackets.

Language focus

1 _____ (go) on a space trip is exciting!

2 _____ (look) at the sky is such fun!

3 _____ (stay) up late is really tiring.

I need to go to bed – it's almost one!

2 Write sentences for the photos.

Eating vegetables is
healthy.

fun.

exciting.

hard.

dangerous.

boring.

3 Write five more sentences about yourself. Use a different adjective in each sentence and the gerund of some of the verbs from the box.

play   watch   cook   help   read   study for a test   tidy   write   do

1 Reading about the moon landing is interesting.

2 _____

3 _____

4 _____

5 _____

6 _____

1 🎧 025 🛡 **Remember the song. Complete the report with the words from the box.**

went   happy   didn't   so   ~~talked~~   stars   radio   about   flying   tired

GROUND CONTROL MISSION LOG: February 1970

When we (1) ___talked___ to Commander Graham this morning, he seemed very
(2) _____. He was enjoying (3) _____ fast and looking at the view.
He really liked watching the (4) _____ come up. Then he was
(5) _____, so he (6) _____ to bed. The next time we called him on
the radio, he (7) _____ answer. Was he sleeping? Was his (8) _____
working? We aren't sure, (9) _____ we're worried (10) _____ him.

2 🎧 026 **Listen and say the words.**

s**u**n   s**o**n   l**o**ve

sun

son

Phonics tip

The *u* sound, as in s**u**n, can be spelled in different ways.

3 **Complete the sentences with the words from the box. Match them with the pictures.**

monkeys   money   doesn't
~~London~~   front   lovely

1 There are so many fun
things to do in ___London___ .

2 The _____ at the zoo
are funny.

3 Gus _____ like running
in the hot sun.

4 My mum's got a _____
new jumper.

5 It's very dangerous to walk in
_____ of a bus at a bus stop.

6 My older cousin gave me some
_____ for my birthday.

e

4 🎧 027 **Listen, check and say the sentences.**

Song practice; phonics focus: different spellings of the sound /ʌ/

1 Complete the reported speech sentences with the past simple of the verbs in brackets.

Language focus

I met an astronaut today.

He said that he (1) ___was___ (be) back from the stars.

He said that he (2) _____ (like) our planet best.

But he said that he (3) _____ (have to) visit Mars.

He said that he (4) _____ (not know) the way.

He said that he (5) _____ (want) a map.

But I said that I (6) _____ (not have) one.

And that's because I'm a cat.

2 Complete the sentences.

1 I really love broccoli soup. → She said that she _really loved broccoli soup_ .

2 I watch TV every night for three hours. → He said that he _____ .

3 I feed the cat every morning at seven. → She said that she _____ .

4 I play football every Saturday afternoon. → He said that he _____ .

5 I take the dog for a walk every evening. → She said that she _____ .

3 Read the interview with Zonrak's friend. Complete the journalist's report.

Journalist So, you're Zonrak's friend Zaprax and you're from Alpha 346 too. Have you got a family?

Zaprax Yes, I've got a wife and two boys.

Journalist Do the children go to school?

Zaprax No, because robots give the children lessons at home.

Journalist What sort of work do you do?

Zaprax I'm a scientist and a pilot.

Journalist So you've got two jobs?

Zaprax Yes, everyone has got two jobs.

Journalist Isn't it difficult to have two jobs?

Zaprax No, it isn't. We only need to sleep for three hours at night.

Yesterday, I talked to Zaprax, another alien from Alpha 346. I asked about his family and he said that he (1) ___had a wife and two boys___ . I was interested to find out about schools on Alpha 346, but Zaprax said that (2) _____ at home. When I asked about his work, Zaprax said that he (3) _____ : he's a scientist and a pilot. I was surprised, but he explained that on Alpha 346, (4) _____ .

This sounded like very hard work to me, but Zaprax said that it (5) _____ difficult because they only (6) _____ for three hours at night.

1 Remember the story. Read and match.

1 The men think that the children are spies and — **h**

2 Suddenly one of the engineers feels dizzy and — ☐

3 Then the security officer sits down and — ☐

4 Soon the whole control room is asleep and the — ☐

5 Phoebe realises that there was something — ☐

6 They hear a voice calling the control room and — ☐

7 The children sit in front of a computer and they — ☐

8 Alex tells Neil what the problem is and — ☐

9 The engineers wake up and — ☐

10 The engineers want to know how Alex did it, — ☐

a children wonder what is happening.

b in their tea.

c put on the headsets.

d so he tells them about Moonlanding 2000.

e he sits down and falls asleep.

f Neil Armstrong tells them how Alex saved the day.

g he helps him to leave the moon.

h ~~they want to lock them up.~~

i they know that they must help Neil Armstrong.

j he falls asleep too.

2 Who do you think says these things?

1 'I'm taking you to my room.'
   the security officer

2 'Why are they all asleep?'
   _____

3 'This is our best chance to escape.'
   _____

4 'Hello … Hello … Is there anyone there?'
   _____

5 'I remember this bit from the game.'
   _____

6 'Why are you wearing my headset?'
   _____

3 Complete the computer game blurb.

MOONLANDING 2000

It's 1969 and you are an (1) engineer
working for NASA in (2) H_____.
In this exciting computer
(3) m_____ f_____
s_____ game, you have to help the
famous (4) a_____
(5) N_____ A_____ and
his crew to bring their
(6) s_____ c_____ safely
back to (7) E_____.

4 Read the sentences in the box. Who said these things in the story? Complete the newspaper article using reported speech.

> I play it all the time.   I feel dizzy.   I'm really good at it.   We need help.   It's a computer game.

STRANGE HAPPENINGS AT NASA

Three mysterious children have saved Neil Armstrong's historic mission from disaster. But who are they? The children were found in the NASA control room. Nobody knew where they came from. The security officer was going to lock them in his room when he said that he (1) ___felt dizzy___ . In the next few minutes, all the NASA engineers fell asleep at their desks. Only the children were awake when Armstrong said over the loudspeakers that they (2) _____. For the next half an hour, one of the boys helped Armstrong and when the engineers woke up, the lunar module was safely off the moon. When the engineers asked the boy how he knew what to do, he said that it (3) _____ called Moonlanding 2000. He said that he (4) _____ and that he (5) _____. The children then walked into a yellow light and disappeared. Humans? Aliens? Ghosts? Will we ever know what really happened?

5 🛡 Which of the four engineers is the spy?

The spy is number _____ because _____ .

1 Complete the email. Write one word in each space.

Dear Lucas,

At the moment, I'm sitting (1) _____on_____ the beach with two alien friends, using their solar-powered laptop! They (2) _____ back with me from our trip in the space capsule. We arrived back on Earth two days (3) _____ and now all three of us (4) _____ very tired. Travelling in space was hard work, (5) _____ it was a lot of fun too. Next week, a tourist is coming (6) _____ us. She's a millionaire and she has (7) _____ $25,000,000 for the trip. First, we're (8) _____ to the aliens' space station on Mars. After (9) _____, we're going to Venus.

I'll (10) _____ lots of photos and send them to you.

Love,

Sophie

2 Complete the interview. Choose the correct letter (A–H). There are two extra answers.

Interviewer   How was your trip?

Space tourist (1) [C]

Interviewer   Did you really land on Venus?

Space tourist (2) [ ]

Interviewer   How much was the flight?

Space tourist (3) [ ]

Interviewer   Would you go again?

Space tourist (4) [ ]

Interviewer   Where would you like to go next?

Space tourist (5) [ ]

Interviewer   Why Saturn?

Space tourist (6) [ ]

A I'm not going to tell you, but believe me, it was very expensive!

B To Saturn.

C ~~It was fantastic!~~

D You're welcome!

E No, I was perfectly fine. I trained 600 hours for this flight.

F Yes, I'd love to. Actually, I've already made plans.

G Because I'd like to study the rings there.

H Of course we did. That's what I paid for!

1 (028) **Listen to the story in the Student's Book again. Write _t_ (true), _f_ (false) or _ds_ (doesn't say).**

1 Leo and Rosy were the two biggest monkeys.   _ds_

2 The control room lost contact with the monkeys on the fourth day.   _____

3 No-one from COSPACE had landed on Pluto before.   _____

4 When the astronauts first landed, they couldn't see any living things. _____

5 The statue of Leo and Rosy was very old.   _____

2 **What message can we learn from the story? Underline the best value statement.**

a Knowing when to say sorry is important.

b Asking people to say sorry is bad.

c Being right is more important than saying sorry.

3 **Look at the pictures and write the end of the story.**

_____

_____

_____

_____

_____

Think and learn

1 Read and complete the sentences.

characters   planets   constellations   burn   the Sun   solar system   ~~gas~~   billion   millions   galaxy

Stars are big, burning balls of (1) _____gas_____ , which are bigger than (2) _____.
They take (3) _____ of years to (4) _____ all the gas inside them.
The closest star to Earth is (5) _____. It is also at the centre of our (6) _____.
A group of stars is called a (7) _____. Ours is called the Milky Way, and it has more
than 100 (8) _____ stars in it. It also has many different (9) _____ –
these are smaller groups of stars that make particular shapes. They are often named after
(10) _____ from stories.

2 🛡 Can you remember? Number the stages of a star's life in the correct order.

A star is created. ☐   We can't see it any more. ☐   A star burns all the gas inside it. ☐

There is a big, cold cloud of gas called a star factory. ☐1   Clouds break up and get very hot. ☐

3 Read and complete the information about stars. Number them in order of temperature
(1 = the hottest).

We know what stars are made of and how they are made, but did you know that there are different
coloured stars? The biggest, hottest stars are blue, like Rigel – the brightest star in the Orion constellation.
Scientists think its surface temperature is around 12,000 degrees Celsius (°C) . At the other end of the scale,
red stars are the coolest (yes, really!), but they are still very hot. For example, Betelgeuse is around
3,200 °C. Between red stars and blue stars are yellow stars, like the Sun, with a temperature of
around 5,500 °C.

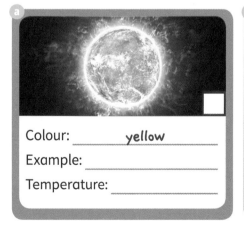

a
Colour: _____yellow_____
Example: _____
Temperature: _____

b
Colour: _____
Example: _____
Temperature: _____

c
Colour: _____
Example: _____
Temperature: _____

4 Match the constellations with their names.

Cancer (the crab) ~~Canis major (the big dog)~~ Draco (the dragon)

Hydra (the water-snake) Pegasus (the flying horse) Pisces (the fishes)

①

Canis major

②

③

④

⑤

⑥

5 Read the descriptions and write the name of a constellation from Activity 4.

1 _____Draco_____ is the eighth-largest constellation in the sky. In Greek mythology, it was a large creature that was killed by the hero, Hercules. You can see its head, which is marked out by four stars, quite clearly at the bottom.

2 _____ represents the Greek goddess Aphrodite and her son, Eros, who changed into fish and jumped into a river to escape from a scary monster. There is a very clear circle of seven stars on one of them.

3 _____ is one of the biggest constellations and is easy to spot because of four very bright stars in a square, which represent the animal's body.

4 _____ contains Sirius, the brightest star in the sky. The constellation is very close to the constellation Orion, named after the hunter in Greek mythology, and it represents one of Orion's hunting animals.

5 _____ is the longest constellation in the whole sky. Its name comes from the snake with many heads in Greek mythology, which Hercules fought. Five stars make up its head, while the rest of its body stretches across the sky.

6 _____ is named after a very minor character from Greek mythology which bit Hercules while he was fighting the multi-headed snake. Unfortunately, someone then stood on it and squashed it. It is made up of six stars.

6 ⭐ Project Find and write the names of three more constellations in English.

_____ _____ _____

1 Make three sentences with the phrases in the diamond.
Use three different phrases in each sentence.

1 Looking _____
_____ .
2 _____
_____ .
3 _____
_____ .

```
                    space is
                    fantastic
            he ate
            carrot ice      I said to the
            cream
   The alien      spoke two
   said that      languages      for breakfast
                          alien that
            Looking       I only
                 at Earth
                 from
```

2 Find the words and use them to complete the sentences.

```
(1)      s
    n       r
      e
    e
      e
```

```
(2)      t
   c       r
     s   a
   r     e
```

```
(3)   a
   t     d
     h   e
   s
     e
```

```
(4)    n
     w   d
   u   o   t
     c n o
```

```
(5)   l  o
   s n   t
    e
   c t   n
    a o l
      i
```

```
(6)     a
     x
   g   l
         y
     a
```

1 The engineers in the control room watched everything on a big _____screen_____ .
2 On the moon you can see lots of _____ .
3 There's something wrong with my _____ , so I can't hear anything.
4 The minutes were ticking away on the _____ clock.
5 A group of stars that makes a pattern in the sky is called a _____ .
6 Our _____ is called the Milky Way.

3 Complete the sentences with your own ideas.

1 The alien said that she liked _____ .
2 Reading _____ .
3 The aliens said that they _____ .
4 Travelling to _____ .

1 What do I know? — Read and tick ✓. Then write examples.

1 I can write sentences with gerunds. ☐

_____

2 I can use reported speech. ☐

_____

3 I can write the names of five things related to the moon landing. ☐

_____ _____ _____

_____ _____

2 Write sentences to answer the Big Question.

BIG QUESTION What do we know about space?

_____

3 My story — Look at the pictures and write the story.

One day, an alien landed ...

_____

8 A cold place

1 Complete the words with the letters on the igloo.

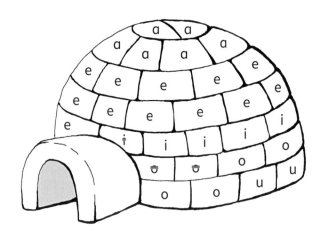

1 _i_ g l _o_ _o_
2 s _ _ _ _ l
3 m _ _ t t _ _ n s
4 _ _ c _ b _ _ r g
5 s l _ _ d g _ _
6 p _ _ l _ _ r b _ _ _ _ r
7 N _ _ r t h _ _ r n   L _ _ g h t s
8 _ _ c _ _   f l _ _ _ _
9 p _ _ l _ _ r   b _ _ _ r   c _ _ b
10 s _ _ _ _ l   p _ _ p

2 Match the definitions with the words from Activity 1.

a [4] a big block of ice in the sea
b [ ] a big, white predator in the Arctic
c [ ] an adult animal that answer **b** likes to eat
d [ ] this slides over the snow
e [ ] the baby of answer **b**

f [ ] a house made of ice bricks
g [ ] the baby of answer **c**
h [ ] you put these on your hands
i [ ] flat ice floating on the sea
j [ ] you see these in the Arctic sky

3 Look at the pictures. Choose the correct form of the words from Activity 1 to complete the story. You don't need to use all the words and you can use some more than once.

Akiak was hunting (1) _____seals_____ in his kayak. He saw one on an (2) _____, so he rowed closer. Suddenly he saw a (3) _____ in the water. It got onto the (4) _____ and the (5) _____ escaped quickly. The (6) _____ looked around and saw Akiak, who then turned the kayak and paddled hard. The (7) _____ jumped into the water and followed him. Akiak's dogs were waiting near the edge of the water with his (8) _____. When he reached the hard ice, he jumped on the sledge and the dogs ran as fast as they could.

1 Read and circle the correct question tags.

Language focus

It's cold at the poles, (1) **is** / **isn't** it?   There isn't much sun there, (3) **is** / **isn't** there?

And the nights are dark, (2) **are** / **aren't** they?   The days aren't long, (4) **are** / **aren't** they?

Great for a polar bear perhaps,   A good place for penguins perhaps,

But not a good place for me.   But I'd better stay away.

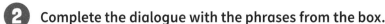

2 Complete the dialogue with the phrases from the box.

> am I   are they   aren't they   aren't they   ~~isn't it~~   isn't it   isn't it   is it

Josh   My grandparents are going to the Arctic on holiday.

Eva   Wow! That's in the north, (1) _____**isn't it**_____?

Josh   Yes, that's right. They want to see the *aurora borealis*.

Eva   The *aurora borealis*? They're the Northern Lights, (2) _____?

Josh   Yes, *aurora borealis* is their scientific name.

Eva   They aren't going to hike to the North Pole, (3) _____?

Josh   No, of course not! They're going on a cruise to the north of Norway, but they will get to do some hiking.

Eva   That's difficult in the snow, (4) _____?

Josh   Yes, but they'll have special snowshoes.

Eva   And Norway's a great place to see whales too, (5) _____?

Josh   Yes, they're hoping to see some whales too.

Eva   It's not great for penguins though, (6) _____?

Josh   Not great? It's impossible! There aren't any penguins there at all.

Eva   Oh dear. I'm not very good at geography (7) _____?

Josh   No, but I'm sure my grandparents can tell you all about it!

Eva   They are really lucky, (8) _____?

3 Complete the sentences with question tags.

1 Alice's favourite food is spaghetti, _____**isn't it**_____?

2 You aren't cold, _____?

3 Peter and Harry are in Year 6, _____?

4 New York isn't the capital of the USA, _____?

5 Mum is very angry about the window, _____?

6 I'm sure you're having a lot of fun, _____?

1 Complete the dialogue with the phrases from the box.

Did you say   are they   Can I just check something   ~~aren't they~~   just remind me   isn't it

Thomas	Hi, Chloe. Our Antarctica projects are due in this week, (1) ___aren't they___ ?
Chloe	Yes, that's right.
Thomas	And (2) _____, Antarctica is the North Pole (3) _____?
Chloe	No, it's the South Pole.
Thomas	Oh, OK. So, it's a place where you find lots of whales … but I can't write about them, can I?
Chloe	Errr … why not?
Thomas	Well, because whales aren't animals, (4) _____?
Chloe	What? (5) _____ whales aren't animals?
Thomas	That's right, they're fish.
Chloe	Oh dear! (6) _____? You're just joking, aren't you? You do really know that whales are mammals, and that mammals and fish are animals?

2 🔊 029 Listen and say the words.

weather   to**day**
holiday   com**pu**ter

What's the <u>wea</u>ther like to<u>day</u>?

It's <u>sun</u>ny.

Phonics tip

In longer words, we need to stress one syllable more than the others.

3 Say the words in the box and write them in the correct syllable stress column.

~~penguin~~ ~~across~~ ~~yesterday~~ ~~adventure~~ mittens
because   problem   remind   grandparents   depends
animal   forgotten   suddenly   tomorrow   finished   decided

● ● **wea**ther	● ● to**day**	● ● ● **ho**liday	● ● ● com**pu**ter
penguin	across	yesterday	adventure

Word watch

The sound in the unstressed syllables is very short. This sound can be spelled in different ways, for example <u>a</u>cross, yest<u>er</u>day and c<u>o</u>mput<u>er</u>.

4 🔊 030 Listen, check and say the words.

1 Read and order. Write numbers 1–8.

Language focus

☐ Don't let this happen, please.

☐ Because people want our trees.

1 The jungle may be in danger

☐ They might take our home away.

☐ There might not be enough to last.

☐ The Arctic may be in trouble.

☐ The ice is melting fast.

☐ Polar bears won't find food.

2 Rewrite the sentences with *may*.

1 Perhaps Lucy's at home now.　　Lucy _may be at home now_ .

2 Perhaps Mum will buy a new car.　　Mum _____ .

3 Perhaps Jack's angry.　　Jack _____ .

4 Perhaps Ella doesn't eat spinach.　　Ella _____ .

5 Perhaps it will be very cold tomorrow.　　It _____ .

6 Perhaps Peter won't want to go.　　Peter _____ .

3 Look at the pictures. Jack is dreaming about the future. Write sentences with *may* or *might* and the verbs from the box.

win　invite　see　get　be　~~ask~~

Mr Hay _might ask me to join the team_ .

Our team _____ .

We _____ .

There _____ .

Jess _____ .

Jess _____ .

1 🛡 **Remember the story. Choose the correct answers.**

This is a seal (1) **baby** / **cub** / **pup.**
Its other name is a (2) **sealcoat** / **whitecoat** / **whiteseal**.

This is a (3) **snow-go** / **snow sledge** / **ski-doo**.
(4) **More than one person** / **Only one person** can ride on it.

2 🛡 **Complete the summary with the missing letters. Each letter of the alphabet is missing once.**
Tick ✔ each letter when you use it in the grid below.

The children see si_x_ seal pups on an ice floe. They are called white___oats. Phoebe tells the others all about them and that they are pr___tected in Canada. They hear a ___oise and they see two men get off a ski-doo. They are carr___ing st___cks because they are coming to ___ill the pups. The children ___ump onto the ice floe and p___sh it out into the sea using their spa___es. The two men try to get on the ice ___loe but they are too la___e. The pups are safe!

However, the children are now f___r from the ___each. They can't get in and swim b___cause the ___ater is free___ing. A ___elicopter appears above them. They wa___e and the pilot sees them. Soon they are all rescued. The children tell the ___ilot about the men and he ___adioes the po___ice ___tation. The police ___uickly find the men and the children help to identify them. After that, they walk back to the beach and see the ___ate in the ___iddle of an ice floe.

a	b	c	d	e	f	g	h	i	j	k	l	m
n	o	p	q	r	s	t	u	v	w	x✓	y	z

3 **Choose the best ending for each sentence.**

1 Phoebe didn't think that they should get closer to the seals because …
   a ☐ it might be dangerous.
   b ✔ the seals might not like it.
   c ☐ she didn't want to get wet.

2 When the men saw what the children were doing …
   a ☐ they jumped into the water.
   b ☐ they tried to get on the ice floe.
   c ☐ they jumped on their ski-doo.

3 The helicopter was out because the pilot was looking for …
   a ☐ the two men.
   b ☐ seals.
   c ☐ the children.

4 When the children got to the police station …
   a ☐ the police were still looking for the men.
   b ☐ a police officer took a photo of them.
   c ☐ they were shown some photos to identify the men.

4 Look at the picture of the men on Student's Book page 98. Complete the dialogue.

Police officer   Can you tell us what the two men looked like?

Phoebe   Yes, one of them had (1) _____dark_____ curly (2) _____ and

a (3) _____ .

Alex   And he was wearing a (4) _____ jacket.

Police officer   And the other one?

Patrick   He had (5) _____ hair and (6) _____ … I think?

Phoebe   Yes, he did. I remember them. He had a (7) _____ on his face and he was

wearing a (8) _____ jacket.

Police officer   Can you look at these photos and identify the men?

Alex   Let me see … yes, this man here.

Patrick   And this one here.

Phoebe   That's them!

5 What message can we learn from the story? <u>Underline</u> the best value statement.

a We need to hunt wild animals to stay safe.

b Hunters should hunt wild animals.

c We must protect wild animals.

turtle dove

6 Read the article and write *t* (true) or *f* (false).

Every year, hundreds of thousands of birds are killed as they make the long journey from Africa to Europe. Birds like turtle doves, nightingales, cuckoos and ospreys spend the European winter on the African continent and they return to Europe in the spring to make nests and lay eggs. In September, they leave again to fly back to Africa, where it is warm. Unfortunately, as these birds fly over the south of Europe and the sea north of Africa, many are shot and killed, even though these birds are protected by international laws. Some are eaten, but most are just shot for fun. This means that these traditional summer birds are becoming much more difficult to find in Europe and experts say that some are in real danger. We must stop this killing now!

nightingale

cuckoo

1 The only birds that are shot are turtle doves, nightingales, cuckoos and ospreys.   [f]

2 The birds spend their lives on three different continents.   [ ]

3 They fly south in September.   [ ]

4 It is illegal to shoot these birds.   [ ]

5 Most of the birds are shot for food.   [ ]

6 It was easier in the past to see birds like cuckoos in Europe.   [ ]

osprey

1 Read and complete the story with the correct words from the box.
There are two words you don't need.

> angry ~~snow~~ drink smell happily kicked barking reindeer tightly crying

One day, an adventurer was hiking in the (1) _____snow_____ with his dog. After hiking for many hours, the man was very thirsty. He looked for a stream to (2) _____ from, but everything was frozen. Then he spotted some water trickling down the ice. The man sat down and took a cup from his bag. The dog started (3) _____, but the man told him to be quiet. He put the cup against the ice to collect the water and he waited for a long time.

When the cup was almost full, he put it to his mouth. At that moment, the dog pushed the cup out of the man's hand. The man was very (4) _____. Again, he put the cup against the ice and waited. As soon as he went to drink from the cup, the dog pushed it out of his hand again. Now the man was really angry. For the third time, he put his cup against the ice. This time he was very careful and held the cup very (5) _____. When he put the cup to his mouth, the dog jumped on him from behind and the cup fell onto the snow. The man was so angry now that he (6) _____ snow at the dog.

He decided to climb up the ice to find where the water was coming from. It was difficult, but when he finally found the small pool of melted water, he knew why the dog was behaving so strangely. There was a dead (7) _____ in the pool. The water was poisonous and the dog could (8) _____ it. The man quickly climbed down and apologised to his dog. He was very thirsty, but also happy. The only reason he was still alive was because dogs have better noses than humans.

2 Now choose the best title for the story. Tick ☑ one box.

Thirsty work ☐ Man kicks dog ☐ Saved by the smell ☐

1 🎧 031 **Listen to Emma talking to James about buying a present for her brother.**
Tick ✓ A, B or C. There is one example.

1 Emma's brother likes to read …
  A science fiction. ☐   B detective stories. ✓   C fairy tales. ☐

2 The book which James has just read is …
  A *The Polar Bear.* ☐   B *The Kites.* ☐   C *The Polar Kids.* ☐

3 The book is about two children who have …
  A no friends. ☐   B run away. ☐   C no aunt. ☐

4 Emma's brother will be …
  A eleven. ☐   B twelve. ☐   C nine. ☐

5 The bookshop is in …
  A Bridge Road. ☐   B Park Lane. ☐   C River Road. ☐

6 The price of the book was …
  A €12. ☐   B €10. ☐   C €22. ☐

2 **Ella and Max are having a conversation about buying equipment for an expedition.**
Read and choose the best answer. Write letters (A–H). There are three extra answers.

Ella Have you got your skis yet? Do you know where I could get some?

Max (1) _____F_____

Ella That sounds good. Where is it?

Max (2) _____

Ella Is it a big shop?

Max (3) _____

Ella Great. Do you know when they close?

Max (4) _____

Ella OK, I'll call them and check. Do you have their number?

Max (5) _____

A I think they're open late most days except Sundays.

B It's on Scott Street, just past the supermarket, on your left.

C Yes, it's www.wintersports.com

D No, but you could look on their website and get it from there.

E No, I haven't. I need to get some.

F ~~Yes, I got mine from The Winter Sports Shop last weekend.~~

G Yes, it's enormous – they've got loads of skis, snowboards and sledges.

H Yes, I love them.

3 **What other questions could Ella ask about the shop? Write two more questions.**

_____

_____

1 **What are they? Look and write the letter.**

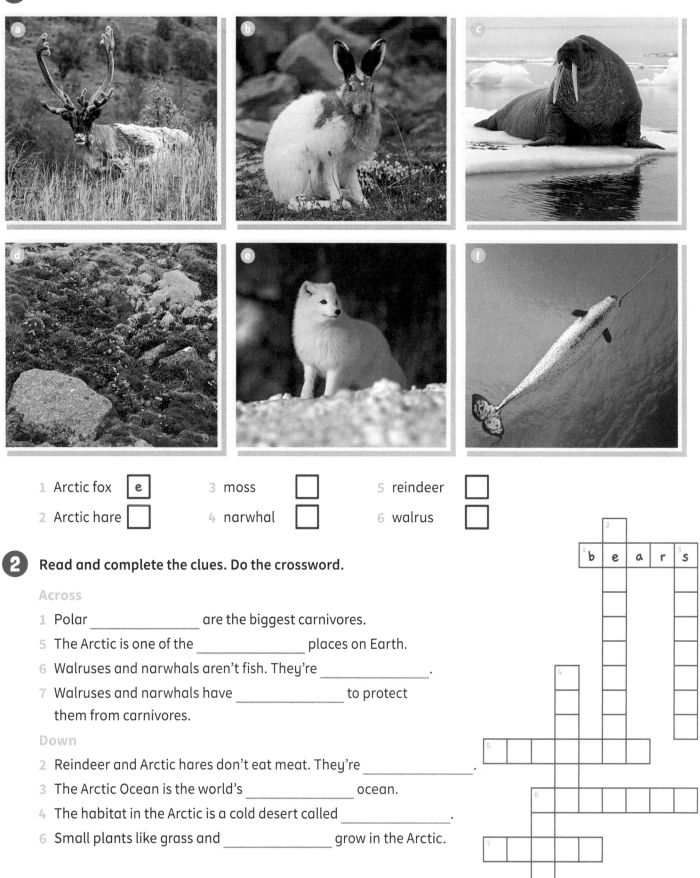

1 Arctic fox ☐ e   3 moss ☐   5 reindeer ☐

2 Arctic hare ☐   4 narwhal ☐   6 walrus ☐

2 **Read and complete the clues. Do the crossword.**

Across

1 Polar _____ are the biggest carnivores.

5 The Arctic is one of the _____ places on Earth.

6 Walruses and narwhals aren't fish. They're _____.

7 Walruses and narwhals have _____ to protect them from carnivores.

Down

2 Reindeer and Arctic hares don't eat meat. They're _____.

3 The Arctic Ocean is the world's _____ ocean.

4 The habitat in the Arctic is a cold desert called _____.

6 Small plants like grass and _____ grow in the Arctic.

Crossword: 1 across: b e a r s

3 You are going to read an article about how plants survive in the Arctic.
Tick ✓ the things that you think might help plants to survive there.

white flowers ☐   shallow roots ☐   big leaves ☐   tall plants ☐

dark flowers ☐   long, deep roots ☐   small leaves ☐   short plants ☐

4 Read the article and check your answers to Activity 3.
<u>Underline</u> the things from Activity 3 that are mentioned in the text.

ARCTIC PLANT LIFE

We've looked at some of the animals and people that live in the Arctic and have seen how they survive there, but what about the plants?

For plants in the Arctic, finding the heat, light and water they need to survive can be a big challenge. The Arctic is in total darkness for about 11 weeks during the winter. But in the middle of summer, it can be light for nearly 24 hours at a time!

Arctic plants can make flowers and seeds very quickly when it's sunny. Many of them have dark flowers to absorb the sun's energy. Some of them also have cup-shaped flowers so that they can direct the sun's energy into the middle of the flower. ☐

Water is only available in the Arctic for a short amount of time too. There are only 50–90 days when the ground isn't covered in ice, and even then, only a very small layer of soil melts enough to provide water. For this reason, Arctic plants have very shallow roots and that's why you won't find trees in the Arctic! You won't find big leaves in the Arctic, either. The plants that survive in the Arctic have very small leaves so that they don't lose much water from the surface.

Arctic plants have also adapted to the cold and windy conditions by staying close to the ground and close to each other. ☐ You won't find many tall plants standing on their own. Many of them also have a thin layer of hair to give them more protection from the wind, ice and snow – just like a woolly jumper! ☐

5 Match the plant photos with the correct part of the text. Write the letter.

6 Write three more characteristics of Arctic plants from the text that are not mentioned in Activity 3.
How do these help the plants to survive?

1 They make flowers and seeds quickly.   3 _____

2 _____   4 _____

7 ⭐ Project   What is the most interesting fact about the Arctic that you found?

❄ _____

1 Choose six words or phrases to complete the sentences.

> haven't   ~~may melt~~   aren't   is   might not   are
>
> may not come   might live   might become   isn't

1 When the weather gets warmer, lots of ice ___may melt___ in the Arctic.
2 Some animals _____ very rare if they can't find food any more.
3 Seals are very good swimmers, _____ they?
4 It _____ rain tomorrow, so we could go camping.
5 Those maps _____ very useful, aren't they?
6 The weather is great today, _____ it?

2 Join the parts to make words and use them to complete the sentences.

> ~~Are~~   mitt   ice   Ant   ig   Nar
>
> berg   whals   ~~tie~~   ens   loo   arctic

1 You'll only find polar bears in the ___Arctic___.
2 Nine-tenths of an _____ is usually under the water, so you can only see a small part of it.
3 _____ are only found in the Arctic Ocean.
4 There are millions of penguins in the _____.
5 Let's quickly build an _____. I think a snowstorm is coming.
6 My hands are cold, so I'm going to put on my _____.

3 Complete the sentences with your own ideas.

1 Your friends are _____, _____?
2 This weekend, I may _____.
3 _____, isn't he?
4 We may _____ next summer.
5 _____, are you?
6 I'm not sure how I will get to your party, but I might _____.

What do I know?

1 Read and tick ✓. Then write examples.

1 I can use question tags with the verb *to be*. ☐

_____

_____

2 I can write sentences with *may / might*. ☐

_____

_____

3 I can write the names of five things found in the Arctic. ☐

_____ _____ _____

_____ _____

2 🛡 Write sentences to answer the Big Question. **BIG QUESTION** What's it like at the Earth's poles?

_____

_____

_____

_____

My letter

3 🛡 Choose an environmental problem. Write a letter for a newspaper. Answer these questions in your letter.

• Why are you writing?

• What may/might/will happen if people don't help?

• What would you like people / the president / the government to do?

STOP KILLING SEALS!

_____

_____

_____

_____

_____

_____

_____

_____

_____

_____

9 The Jurassic Age

1 Do the crossword.

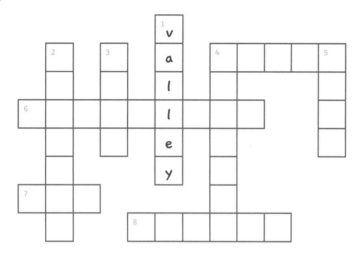

Down
1. ~~This is the land between two mountains.~~
2. This is where the land meets the sky.
3. This is a type of plant with lots of leaves.
4. This is the time in the morning when we first see light.
5. This is a very small lake or pool.

Across
4. This is very wet muddy land.
6. This is a place with lots of grass.
7. This is a cylinder of wood from a tree.
8. This is a small river.

2 Write the words from Activity 1. Add other words that you know.

1. Words connected with water: _____pond_____ , _____ , _____
   Can you add any more? _____
2. Words connected with plants and trees: _____ , _____ , _____
   Can you add any more? _____
3. Words connected with the sky: _____ , _____
   Can you add any more? _____

3 Complete the dialogue with the words from the box.

> past   dinosaur   swamp   joking   future   pond   ~~strange~~   horizon

Alex   Wow, this place is (1) _____strange_____ ! Any idea where we are?

Patrick   Look at that muddy (2) _____ . I've never seen anywhere like it. I think we're in the
          (3) _____ .

Phoebe   No, I think we're in the (4) _____ . I think we're in a time before people walked
          on Earth.

Patrick   Why do you think that?

Phoebe   Well, if you look over there on the (5) _____ , I think there's a (6) _____ .

Alex   A dinosaur? You're (7) _____ !

Patrick   She isn't. Look over there by the (8) _____ . There are some dinosaurs feeding.

1 Read and match.

Language focus

1 If I had a time machine, ————— I'd say, 'Well, how are you?'

2 But if I saw a dinosaur, I'd go back to the past.

3 If I had a time machine, I'd come back very fast.

4 And if I met the future me, I'd visit the future too.

2 Complete the sentences with the correct form of the verbs in brackets.

1 If I _____had_____ (have) a lot of money, I'd spend my holiday in the jungle.

2 If I _____ (go) into the jungle, I'd take a camera with me.

3 If I _____ (have) a hot air balloon, I'd fly above the trees.

4 If I _____ (see) a jaguar, I'd take a photo.

5 If I _____ (come) to a river, I'd swim in it.

6 If I _____ (find) a snake, I'd leave it alone.

7 If I _____ (be) tired, I'd sleep in a hammock.

3 Look at the pictures and write sentences with *If I*.

If I had a rocket, I'd fly
to Mars.

_____

_____

_____

_____

1 🎧 032 Listen. Match the song phrases with the definitions. Then match them with the pictures.

1 to hang out   [c]   a to push your finger (or horn!) in someone

2 to mess about   [ ]   b to walk up quietly behind

3 to poke   [ ]   c ~~to spend time (not doing anything special)~~

4 to creep up on   [ ]   d to have fun doing silly things

w [ ]   x [1]   y [ ]   z [ ]

2 🎧 033 Listen and say the words.

sh**or**t **aw**ful b**a**ll dinos**au**r

Phonics tip
There are different ways
of spelling the *or* sound.

an awfully big dinosaur

3 Complete the sentences with the words from the box. Match them with the pictures.

| dinosaurs   small   walking   autumn   ~~tall~~   stories |

1 Are you short or _____ tall _____?   [b]

2 Do you prefer lions or _____?   [ ]

3 Do you prefer summer or _____?   [ ]

4 Would you like a big piece of cake or a
_____ one?   [ ]

5 Do you prefer running or _____?   [ ]

6 Do you usually read _____
that are fact or fiction?   [ ]

4 🎧 034 Listen and check. Ask and answer with a partner.

Song practice; phonics focus: different spellings of the sound /ɔː/ and question intonation

1 Complete with the words from the box.

I'd   If   do   say   ~~would~~   wouldn't   What   met

Language focus

What (1) _____would_____ you do,

(2) _____ would you (3) _____ ,

(4) _____ you saw a dinosaur

Coming your way?

If I (5) _____ a dinosaur,

I know what I would (6) _____ .

I (7) _____ stop to say 'hello',

(8) _____ run and so would you.

2 What would Paul do if … ? Write questions, then match the answers with the questions.

1 __What would Paul do if__
   __he saw__ a thief in a shop?

2 _____
   _____ to New York?

3 _____
   _____ a cat in a tree?

4 _____
   _____ Rafa Nadal?

5 _____
   _____ to Rio de Janeiro?

6 _____
   _____ a new skateboard?

a [ ] He'd go to Central Park.

b [ ] He'd go to the carnival.

c [1] He'd call the police.

d [ ] He'd climb the tree and save it.

e [ ] He'd practise a lot.

f [ ] He'd say 'Hello'.

1 Match the dinosaur names with the pictures.

T-rex   velociraptor   pterosaur   ~~triceratops~~

1 _____triceratops_____   2 _____   3 _____   4 _____

2 Remember the story. Read the summary and complete the words.

The children see a triceratops eating
(1) _____bushes_____ . Alex walks towards it.
Phoebe says that he might (2) s_____ it.
The dinosaur quickly walks away, but it's not Alex
who is scaring it. It's a (3) g_____ of small
dinosaurs which are coming out of the jungle. Patrick
says that they don't need to (4) w_____
because the dinosaurs are only small. Then one of them
opens its (5) m_____ and shows lots of sharp
(6) t_____. Alex knows that they are
velociraptors and he knows that he is in trouble as they
make a (7) c_____ around him. Suddenly,
a huge (8) h_____ appears and grabs one of
the small dinosaurs, so the others run away.
The children are now safe from the velociraptors, but
in big (9) d_____ from a T-rex! They start to
run and just as the huge (10) d_____ is going
to catch them, they are picked up by a pterosaur in its
(11) b_____. The flying dinosaur takes the
children back to its (12) n_____ and drops
them towards its (13) h_____ babies. Luckily,
the gate appears and takes the Time Travellers back to
the safety of their (14) c_____ .

3 Answer the questions.

1 Why does Patrick think that Alex is mad?
   Because he walks towards the
   triceratops.

2 Why isn't Alex scared of the triceratops?
   _____
   _____

3 What are the velociraptors doing when
   the T-rex appears?
   _____
   _____

4 What does the T-rex do when the
   pterosaur picks up the children?
   _____
   _____

5 What does Mr Davis ask the children?
   _____
   _____

6 What does Patrick find in his pocket?
   _____
   _____

4 How much do you remember about the Time Travellers' adventures? Do the quiz.

The GREAT BIG Time Travellers' Quiz

1 What knocks over the jar and causes the explosion which starts the children on their adventures again?
- a Patrick's cap ☐
- b Patrick's goggles ☐
- c Patrick's pen ☐

2 What treasure do the children dig up on the island?
- a Diamonds ☐
- b Bracelets ☐
- c Gold coins ☐

3 What colour buttons open the parachute on the jet pack?
- a Yellow and blue ☐
- b Red and orange ☐
- c Purple and green ☐

4 What creature lands on Phoebe's head inside the pyramid?
- a A scorpion ☐
- b A spider ☐
- c A snake ☐

5 What sport are the children watching when Patrick hurts his foot?
- a Boxing ☐
- b Fencing ☐
- c Wrestling ☐

6 What do the children help Mr Fisher put on his cart when they are escaping from The Great Fire of London?
- a A table ☐
- b A chest ☐
- c Some chairs ☐

7 What does Professor Potts' Homework Express give as the answer to 2,345 x 4,567?
- a New York ☐
- b London ☐
- c Paris ☐

8 What are the NASA engineers all drinking when they fall asleep?
- a Tea ☐
- b Coffee ☐
- c Hot chocolate ☐

9 What rescues the children in the North Pole?
- a A boat ☐
- b A ski-doo ☐
- c A helicopter ☐

10 What scares the triceratops?
- a A T-rex ☐
- b Some velociraptors ☐
- c A pterosaur ☐

Check back through the stories in the Student's Book. Give yourself a point for each answer that you remembered correctly.

ARE YOU READY TO BE A TIME TRAVELLER?

0–3 POINTS Oh dear! You didn't remember very much. You've forgotten almost as much as Phoebe, Alex and Patrick! You need to read the stories again before you can go time travelling.

4–7 POINTS Not bad, but you still need a bit more practice. Read the stories again and you should be ready for time-travelling adventures.

8–10 POINTS Brilliant! You're ready for time travelling now. Be careful in your next Science lesson!

1 Complete the fact files with the animal names and words from the box.

green turtle   ~~bee~~   platypus   cockroach   lays eggs   appeared about 100 million years ago   hibernates
famous for surviving   has a beak   lives in warm seas   a fossil was found in amber   used to be bigger

❶ FACT FILE

Animal: _____ bee _____
Fact 1: _____
Fact 2: _____

❷ FACT FILE

Animal: _____
Fact 1: _____
Fact 2: _____

❸ FACT FILE

Animal: _____
Fact 1: _____
Fact 2: _____

❹ FACT FILE

Animal: _____
Fact 1: _____
Fact 2: _____

2 Read the article on Student's Book page 112 again. Which animal is it?

1 This animal lives in Australia.   ___platypus___
2 It's very hard to find fossils of this animal.   _____
3 This animal is more than 100 million years older than the first dinosaurs.   _____
4 When it's too hot, this animal makes a hole in the mud.   _____
5 Scientists think this animal first appeared around 100 million years ago.   _____
6 This is a mammal that spends a lot of time in water.   _____
7 This animal lives in warm seas all over the world.   _____
8 Scientists think this could be the last animal left on Earth.   _____

3 What message can we learn from the article in the Student's Book? <u>Underline</u> the best value statement.

a The world around us is dangerous.
b The world around us is wonderful.
c The world around us is boring.

1 Lucy's dad asked her about the fossil-hunting trip. Read and choose the best answer. Write letters (A–E).

Dad   So how was the trip, Lucy?

Lucy   (1) _E_

Dad   Oh dear. What went wrong?

Lucy   (2) ___

Dad   Why not?

Lucy   (3) ___

Dad   Ah … yes, I saw them in the kitchen when I came home.

Lucy   (4) ___

Dad   So, you're hungry. OK, I'll cook you your favourite dinner.

Lucy   (5) ___

> A Chris offered me one of his, but I don't like ham.
> B Pizza! Dad, you're the best!
> C Because I left my sandwiches at home.
> D Everything. For a start, I didn't have any lunch.
> E ~~Oh Dad, it was terrible.~~

2 You are going to listen to some information about a type of fossil. Look at the pictures and tick ✓ the statements you think will be true.

1 Ammonites lived in the sea. ☐

2 Ammonites lived on land. ☐

3 Ammonites had spines. ☐

4 Ammonites lived in shells. ☐

5 Whales are related to ammonites. ☐

6 Octopuses are related to ammonites. ☐

Ammonite fossil

3 035 Listen and check your answers to Activity 2. Then listen again and complete the fact file.

Name of fossil: Ammonite

Lived between: (1) ____240____ and (2) _____ million years ago.

Hard or soft bodies? (3) _____

Used to eat: (4) _____ and (5) _____

Used to get eaten by: large sea (6) _____

Artist's idea of how ammonites looked

1 **Look, read and complete.**

> axe berries flint hunt gather weapons ~~woolly mammoth~~

1 ___woolly mammoth___   2 _____   3 _____   4 _____

The Stone Age is called the Stone Age because people used stone to make tools and (5) _____,
like axes with flint heads, at that time. For food, they used to (6) _____ animals and
(7) _____ fruit, berries, leaves and eggs.

2 🛡 **Read more about the Stone Age. Write the phrases in the correct place in the chart.**

Archaeologists divide the Stone Age into different stages. Over time,
many parts of human life – not just tools and weapons – developed
and changed.

In the Old Stone Age, people lived mainly in caves, then in wooden huts.
Later in the Stone Age, houses were stronger. Some had stone or mud
walls and permanent roofs made from dried grass.

Why was that? Well, people developed tools which helped them to chop
down trees, so they started to clear areas of land to grow simple crops
and vegetables. This meant they could stay in one place, rather than
moving around to hunt and gather food. Sometimes they kept cows,
sheep and pigs, for their milk, wool and meat.

During the Stone Age, people also learned how to use fire. At first, they used it for warmth and
protection. By the New Stone Age, they were also using fire for cooking, often in clay pots that they
had made. Many New Stone Age houses had an area inside for a fire – a kind of Stone Age kitchen!

> ~~hunting and gathering~~   fire for protection
>
> stone or mud houses with grass roofs
>
> caves or wooden huts
>
> growing crops and keeping animals
>
> fire for cooking

	Old Stone Age	New Stone Age
Homes		
Food and farming	hunting and gathering	
Fire		

9

3 Read about another development in the Stone Age. Write *t* (true), *f* (false) or *ds* (doesn't say).

Stone Age Art

Hunter-gatherers often painted the inside of their caves. The oldest cave paintings date from around 40,000 years ago and were found in Australia. The oldest cave paintings in Europe are around 28,000 years old. There are lots of cave paintings in the south-west of France and the north of Spain. Cave paintings have also been found in parts of Asia and Africa.

Stone Age people used the earth around them to make paint. Yellow paint came from clay, red paint from stones and black paint from charcoal. The natural colours were mixed with water and then painted onto cave walls with fingers or brushes which were made from fur, feathers or twigs.

Cave paintings show the natural world that Stone Age people saw around them. They might be maps or messages about natural features, time or distance. Many paintings show animals, but some show groups of simple 'stick people' hunting, or perhaps the stars in the night sky.

1 Cave paintings have been found in several continents. _____t_____
2 The oldest cave paintings in the world are in France. _____
3 Blue was never used in cave paintings. _____
4 Cave art was always painted with paintbrushes. _____
5 Stone Age people used parts of plants and animals to paint with. _____
6 Cave paintings never show rivers or trees. _____

4 Look. What do you think these cave paintings mean? Write a letter.

a I've found a new cave in the forest.
c It's raining on the other side of the mountain.
b Be careful! There are lots of buffalo over the hill.

5 Project Choose one of the ideas below and draw a cave painting for it.

• There are lots of fish in the lake in the forest.
• Follow the path this way to the river.
• I caught a reindeer today.

1 Draw lines and complete the sentences with the words from the box.

if you had   do if   I'd go   ~~buy an~~   If I   I were

1 If I had a	a time machine, _____	in a film about dinosaurs.
2 If I had	you _____	to the year 2166.
3 _____ had a telescope,	lot of money, I'd	stars every night.
4 Where would you	an actor, I'd like to be	_____ a plane?
5 If _____	fly	you saw a dinosaur?
6 What would	I'd look at the	_buy an_ amazing new computer.

2 Find the words and use them to complete the sentences.

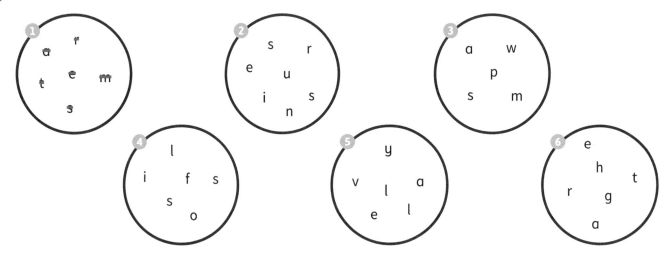

1 We sat down and had a picnic near a lovely _____ stream _____ where there were lots of fish.

2 We left the campsite shortly after _____.

3 Don't go near that _____ because there are crocodiles in it.

4 You can see a _____ of an ammonite in this stone.

5 The river flows down the mountain and into the _____ below.

6 We went into the field to _____ eggs.

3 Complete the sentences with your own ideas.

1 Where would you _____?

2 If I were _____, _____.

3 What _____ had _____?

4 If I had a superpower, _____.

5 What would _____ met _____?

6 If I were _____, _____ every day.

What do I know?

1 Read and tick ☑. Then write examples.

1 I can write sentences with the 2nd conditional. ☐

_____

_____

2 I can write questions with the 2nd conditional. ☐

_____

_____

3 I can write the names of five natural features. ☐

_____ _____ _____

_____ _____

2 🛡 Write sentences to answer the Big Question.

BIG QUESTION What do we know about prehistoric times?

_____

_____

_____

_____

My story

3 🛡 Look at the pictures and write the story.

The time machine was ready.

_____

_____

_____

_____

_____

_____

_____

_____

_____

1 A blog entry

Tips for writers

- When you write on the Internet, don't give any information that shows people *exactly* who you are and *exactly* where you live, go to school or spend your free time. People can use this information to hurt you.
- Use a second verb without the 'little words' (*I, he, she, 've, 's, 'm, going to, can*) to give more information in fewer words:
  *I've joined a team **and played** a match.*
  *I can speak **and write** English.*
  *She's going to come **and play** too.*

1 Tick ☑ three safe things to write on the Internet. Cross ☒ the three things that you shouldn't write.

1 My friends call me Footiefan. ☑

2 Mum's the headteacher at Ely School. ☐

3 I go to Art Club on Mondays. ☐

4 The party's at my house: 4 Mill Lane, York! ☐

5 My best friend is in class 7B. ☐

6 I go to Cross Street Tennis Club on Fridays at 4.15. ☐

2 Complete the sentences with the verbs from the box.

~~did~~ given ~~joined~~ listening play

1 I've started swimming and ___joined___ a club.

2 Dan went home and _____ his homework.

3 I'm reading and _____ to music.

4 She's going to sing and _____ the violin.

5 He's finished his project and _____ it to Mrs Tate.

3 Imagine you are a new student in Phoebe, Alex and Patrick's class. Write a blog entry. Include the points below, but you can also invent information and use your own ideas. Remember to join verbs in one sentence without the little words.

- Safe information about yourself
- Two things that you have done since you started at the new school
- How the explosion happened in your last Science class

Check your writing

- Is all your information safe? _____
- Did you join verbs without little words to make longer sentences? _____

2 A questionnaire

- When you write a questionnaire, make sure that people know how to answer your questions. For example, do they circle or write words?

- If you ask people to use numbers, remember to explain what they mean.

1 Match the questions with the problems.

1 Should we build a monorail in our city, or would you prefer to use a unicycle?
Yes / No

2 Why haven't you bought a floating skateboard?

_____

3 Did you buy inline skates because they weren't expensive?
Yes ☐ No ☐

4 Number these types of transport from 1–3.
Surfboard ☐ Unicycle ☐
Hang-glider ☐

5 Who is your favourite Time Traveller?
Write the first letter of his/her name. ☐

a ☐ If the person has bought this gadget, they can't answer this.

b ☐ It doesn't explain what the numbers mean.

c [1] There are two questions here.

d ☐ Two of the names start with the same letter.

e ☐ If the person hasn't bought this gadget, they can't answer this.

2 Complete and answer the questions.

1 <u>Would you</u> prefer to use a monorail or a unicycle? **monorail / unicycle**

2 Have _____ a floating skateboard? Why? / Why not? _____

3 Did _____ inline skates? Why? / Why not?

Yes Cheap. ☐   I liked them. ☐

No Expensive. ☐ I didn't like them. ☐

4 Number the types of transport 1–3
(1 = _____).
Surfboard ☐ Unicycle ☐ Hang-glider ☐

3 Write a transport questionnaire. Use different question types.

_____
_____
_____
_____
_____
_____
_____
_____
_____
_____

- How many different question types did you use? _____

- Swap questionnaires with a partner. Can your partner answer yours? _____

3 An invitation

Tips for writers

- When you send an invitation, make sure you give people all the information they need: the date and time, and the place where the party is going to be.
- If you want people to dress up, let them know the theme.
- Don't forget to include your name, so people know who to reply to.

1 Look at the two invitations and tick ☑ the correct options.

To (1) Friday ☐ Sophie ☑ My house ☐

Date: (2) August 10th ☐ tomorrow ☐
6.30–9p.m. ☐

Time: (3) Saturday ☐ till late ☐
7–8.30p.m. ☐

Place: (4) My house ☐ 38 Croxall Close ☐
a pizza restaurant ☐

From: (5) Ellie ☐ Tuesday ☐ December ☐

To (6) Dan ☐ Ancient Rome ☐ Sunday ☐

When: (7) this weekend ☐ March 28th, 3p.m. ☐
November ☐

Where: (8) a cinema ☐ Harry ☐
6 Sidney Street ☐

Theme: (9) Sam ☐ Your hero ☐ Monday ☐

From: (10) tomorrow ☐ September ☐ Ben ☐

2 Imagine you are going to plan a surprise party for a friend's birthday. Look at the list of possible ideas. Circle all the places. Underline all the themes.

○	April 23rd or 30th?	Favourite game character
○	from 6 p.m.	Our house – 19 Andrews Street
○	May 6th/7th?	3.30–5.30 p.m.
○	Headington Village Hall	Space travel
○	May 13th?	10 a.m.–Midday
○	Riverside Pool	Sirens & Pirates
○	May 20th?	2–4 p.m.
○	Green Road Park	Sports!

3 Design and write an invitation. Use the ideas in Activity 2 or your own ideas.
Make it as fun as possible.

Check your writing

Have you included:

the date? _____ , the time? _____ ,
the place? _____ , your name? _____ ,
any special details? _____

4 An email to complain

- When you write to complain, use polite phrases such as *Please could you … ?*
- Explain the problem clearly.

1 Read Clare's email. What is wrong with it? Complete the sentences with the words from the box.

> polite   hasn't   when

Dear Sportshoe World,
The trainers in your online shop are terrible.
I want my money. I won't use your shop again.

---

1 She _____ explained the problem.

2 She hasn't said _____ she bought the trainers.

3 Her email isn't _____.

2 Clare's sister wrote a better email.
Find phrases in the email that mean the same as the phrases below.

Dear Sportshoe World,
I'm writing to complain about some trainers which I bought from your online shop on 13th July.
There is a hole in one of them, so I would like to return them for a refund of €39.99.
Please could you contact me with details about how to return faulty items?
Many thanks for your help.
Katy Curtis

---

1 send them back to the shop: _____

2 when a shop gives you money: _____

3 things that aren't right: _____

3 You can ask for other things too.
Match the requests to the definitions.

I would like to return them in exchange …

1 for a replacement pair.

2 for a voucher. ☐

3 for a pair of Go! trainers, number 4507, black, size 3. ☐

a a different pair of trainers

b a pair of the same trainers

c a kind of 'money' which you can use in a shop

4 Write an email to complain.

You bought the game Basketball Mad from Toys4You last week. One of the hoops is broken. Ask for a refund, a new hoop or a different sports game.

_____
_____
_____
_____
_____
_____
_____
_____
_____
_____
_____
_____

- Swap emails with a partner. Does your partner think yours is polite? _____

5 A postcard

- When you write postcards, use informal language to show your feelings.

  Use exclamations sometimes (not always whole sentences with verbs): *Amazing!*

  Add comments in brackets or use dashes:
  The hotel is great (fab food) and …
  There's a theme park too – brilliant!

- Put the day or date and then use words like *today / tomorrow / yesterday*.

1 Read the postcard. Are the expressions positive 😊 or negative 😖 ?

1 gross ☹
2 rocks ☐
3 lame ☐
4 awesome ☐

Tues 21st

Hi Joe,

I'm writing this on the beach. The sea's warm, but guess what? I found half a burger in the water. Gross or what! There are two theme parks here – this place rocks! Tomorrow we're going to see the castle (Dad's lame idea … BORING!), but the day after that, we're going to the water park. Awesome! I love water parks. See you at school … only two weeks now.

George

2 Read the postcard again and complete the sentences.

1 George is visiting the castle on _____.
2 He's going to the water park on _____.
3 They start school in _____.

3 Write two postcards: one from a school trip to someone in your family and one from a family holiday to a school friend. Use informal language, comments and time phrases.

- Did you use all the expressions from Activity 1? _____
- What time phrases did you use? _____
- How many exclamations and comments did you add? _____

6 A story

Tips for writers

- When you use direct speech in a story, use different verbs to make your story interesting.

- Verbs like *said* can go **before** or **after** a name or a noun:
  'Yes, it can,' said Professor Potts.
  'Yes, it can,' the professor said.

  The verb always goes **after** a pronoun:
  'Yes, it does,' she said.
  ~~'Yes, it does,' said she.~~

- Use speech marks and commas, but don't add commas after question marks or exclamation marks:
  'Oh no!' she exclaimed.

1 Complete the story with the words from the box.
Underline twelve verbs of speech.

> button   doesn't   French   quietly   ~~robot~~   story

B *I* U ☰ ☰ ☰ ☰

'Meet my amazing **(1)** _____robot_____!' the professor <u>exclaimed</u>.
'Can it help me with my homework?' asked Hannah.
'Certainly,' replied the professor. 'Robotolot is the most amazing robot in the world,' he boasted.
'That's great,' explained Hannah, 'because I need to write a **(2)** _____ in French and I'm not very good at it.'
'No problem. Robotolot will help you,' the professor promised and he pressed a **(3)** _____ on his incredible robot.
'GREETINGS, HUMAN GIRL! WHAT IS YOUR NAME?' said the robot.
'Je m'appelle Hannah,' answered Hannah. Then she whispered **(4)** _____ to the professor, 'I'm answering in **(5)** _____.'
'WHAT IS YOUR NAME?' repeated the robot.
'Je m'appelle Hannah!' she laughed.
'WHAT IS YOUR ... ,' but there was a whirring sound as the professor turned it off again.
'Oh dear,' sighed the professor. 'Robotolot **(6)** _____ speak French.'

🔟

2 Complete these verbs from the story.

1 r <u>e</u> <u>p</u> <u>e</u> <u>a</u> <u>t</u> <u>e</u> <u>d</u>
2 b __ __ __ __ __
3 p __ __ __ __ __ __ __
4 s __ __ __ __ __
5 r __ __ __ __ __ __ __
6 l __ __ __ __ __ __

3 Write a story about a machine.
Use ideas from the Student's Book or Workbook (page 73), or your own ideas. Include different verbs of speech.

_____
_____
_____
_____
_____
_____
_____
_____
_____
_____
_____
_____
_____
_____
_____
_____

Check your writing

- How many different verbs of speech did you use? _____
- Did you use commas and speech marks correctly? _____

7 A post on a discussion forum

1 Read the posts and answer the questions.

Author	**Space exploration**
Wonder 1	Yes, I'm in favour of exploring space. Finding out about other planets, for example Mars, helps us to understand our planet, Earth.
Lizard	In my opinion, it's a waste of money. My dad said that they sent something called Beagle 2 to Mars in 2003, but it never made contact with Earth and now they can't find it! $45 million! We shouldn't spend all that money when people on Earth have serious problems, such as not having enough food.
Digger	Yeah, like me! I'm really hungry …
Geddit	Digger, go and watch TV if you can't say anything useful. This is a serious topic. If you ask me, projects like trying to find water on Mars are a waste of time. How can it help?
Kencan	Because if they find water, it means that things could live on Mars. I think it's an amazing idea.

1 Who agrees with space exploration?

_____

2 Who doesn't agree?

_____

3 Whose post is a waste of time?

_____

2 Use the opinion phrases to write sentences with gerunds.

1 (learn / about other planets)

I'm __in__ __favour__ __of__ __learning__ __about other planets.__

2 (help / people on Earth / more important)

In _____ _____, _____
_____
_____ .

3 (send / rockets into space / a waste of money)

_____ you _____ _____ ,
_____
_____ .

3 Choose a new topic that interests you. Write a post for or against. Use phrases from the forum posts and gerunds.

_____
_____
_____
_____
_____
_____
_____
_____
_____
_____

Check your writing

- Which opinion phrases did you use?

_____

- Did you spell the gerunds correctly?

_____

Tips for writers

- When you write a review, describe the **setting** (where the film takes place) and the **characters**. Then introduce the **plot** (some of the things that happen), using the present not the past.

- Don't tell the reader the most important things that happen in the film. Ask one or more questions and invite people to find out for themselves:

  ~~The monster is killed.~~ ➜ *Will they kill it? Watch and find out!*

1 Complete Abby's review with the words from the box.

> because   can't   cartoon   characters
> fall   find   love   outside   penguins   ~~place~~

B I U ☰ ☰ ☰ ☰

The film *Madagascar* starts in New York, but most of the action takes (1) _____**place**_____ on the island of Madagascar, in Africa.

It's a (2) _____ and the main (3) _____ are animals: Marty the zebra, Alex the lion, Melman the giraffe, Gloria the hippo, four penguins and two chimpanzees. They leave the zoo (4) _____ Marty wants to see the world, but they are caught by humans and sent to Africa on a ship. The (5) _____ take control of the ship because they want to go to Antarctica, but the big boxes that contain the animals (6) _____ off the ship and they arrive in Madagascar.

I (7) _____ this film because the voices and the characters are very funny. My favourite scene is when Melman tries and tries, but he (8) _____ get out of his box on the beach in Madagascar!

Does life (9) _____ the zoo change the animals? Watch and (10) _____ out! 📎

2 Write a review of a film that you like. <u>Underline</u> phrases in Abby's review that you can use.

B I U ☰ ☰ ☰ ☰

_____
_____
_____
_____
_____
_____
_____
_____
_____
_____
_____
_____
_____
_____ 📎

Check your writing

- Are the verbs in the present tense?

  _____

- Check all your verbs for *he*, *she* and *it*. Did you remember the -*s*?

  _____

- If a classmate wrote about the same film, compare your ideas.

9 A limerick

1 This kind of short poem is called a limerick. Say the poem and <u>underline</u> the syllables with stresses. The numbers (in brackets) show you how many.

1 There <u>was</u> a young <u>wo</u>man called <u>Sue</u> (3) ✓✓✓
2 Who had a nice day at the zoo. **(3)**
3 She saw <u>hip</u>pos and <u>bats</u> **(2)** ✓✓
4 And lots of big cats **(2)**
5 And she fed all the elephants too! **(3)**

2 Think about the rhythm of a limerick.

1 Look at _hippos_ in line 3. Tick ☑ two other animals that you could use here.
   toucans ☐ giraffes ☐ rhinos ☐
2 Look at _elephants_ in line 5. ~~Cross out~~ the two animals that you **can't** use here.
   kangaroos   crocodiles   anacondas

3 Look at line 1. Write three phrases with the same rhythm as _a young woman_.

___a good teacher___ , _____ ,
_____ , _____

4 Limericks have two rhyme patterns. Which lines rhyme? Write the numbers.

Lines __1__ , _____ and _____ rhyme.
Lines _____ and _____ rhyme.

5 Limerick writers invent funny names to make the lines rhyme. Complete the opening lines of these limericks with food and drink words.

1 There was a professor called Weeze
  Who ate lots of very old ___cheese___ ...
2 There was a young schoolboy from Hakes
  Who said he could make lovely _____ ...
3 There was a strange artist called Doffy
  Who painted his pictures with _____ ...
4 There was an old poet from Drickin
  Who spent all her money on _____ ...

6 Read about Lee. Write a limerick. Use Activity 1 to help you.

Lee was a young schoolboy who went for a swim, where he saw amazing things in the sea, like dolphins, whales and snails. He got home at 3.15.

_____
_____
_____
_____
_____

7 Write a limerick. Follow the rules.

_____
_____
_____
_____
_____

Verb	Past	Past participle
be	was/were	been
become	became	become
begin	began	begun
break	broke	broken
bring	brought	brought
build	built	built
buy	bought	bought
catch	caught	caught
choose	chose	chosen
come	came	come
cost	cost	cost
creep	crept	crept
cry	cried	cried
cut	cut	cut
die	died	died
dig	dug	dug
do	did	done
draw	drew	drawn
drink	drank	drunk
drive	drove	driven
eat	ate	eaten
fall	fell	fallen
feed	fed	fed
feel	felt	felt
fight	fought	fought
find	found	found
fly	flew	flown
forget	forgot	forgotten
get	got	got
get up	got up	got up
give	gave	given
go	went	been*
grow	grew	grown
hang	hung	hung
have got	had	had
hear	heard	heard
hide	hid	hidden
hit	hit	hit
hold	held	held
hurt	hurt	hurt
keep	kept	kept
know	knew	known
lay	laid	laid

Verb	Past	Past participle
leave	left	left
let	let	let
lie	lay	lain
lose	lost	lost
make	made	made
mean	meant	meant
meet	met	met
pay	paid	paid
put	put	put
read	read	read
ride	rode	ridden
ring	rang	rung
run	ran	run
say	said	said
see	saw	seen
sell	sold	sold
send	sent	sent
set	set	set
shine	shone	shone
shrink	shrank	shrunk
sing	sang	sung
sit	sat	sat
sleep	slept	slept
speak	spoke	spoken
spend	spent	spent
spin	span	spun
spread	spread	spread
stand	stood	stood
steal	stole	stolen
stick	stuck	stuck
sweep	swept	swept
swim	swam	swum
take	took	taken
teach	taught	taught
tell	told	told
think	thought	thought
throw	threw	thrown
understand	understood	understood
wake up	woke up	woken up
wear	wore	worn
win	won	won
write	wrote	written

* We also use *gone*.

I've been to Mars. = I've visited Mars.   *He's gone to Mars.* = He's still on Mars!